The. Race. Of. Your. Life!

How to reach retirement secure enough to dote on your grandkids (if you like them), or buy a flat screen TV (if you don't!)

Darryl Rosen

Second Edition
Drose & Associates
Deerfield, IL

The. Race. Of. Your. Life! How to reach retirement secure enough to dote on your grandkids (if you like them), or buy a flat screen TV (if you don't!). Second Edition.
Copyright © 2021 by Darryl Rosen.

All rights reserved.

Printed in the United States of America.

Published by Drose & Associates, Publishing Company, 1052 Central Avenue, Suite 200, Deerfield, IL 60015.

First printing May 2017.

ISBN: 978-1-690-77787-8

Fonts used for title page: Lucida Sans, Corbel
Font used for heading text: Tahoma
Font used for text: Palantino Linotype

Other Books by Darryl Rosen:

SURVIVING THE MIDDLE MILES
26.2 Ways to Cross the Finish Line with Your Customers

WINNING THE CUSTOMER LOYALTY MARATHON
How to Achieve Sales and Service Excellence in the Beverage Business

UNLEASHING YOUR INNER SALES COACH
How to Inspire, Motivate and "Coach" Your Sales Team to Success

TABLE FOR THREE?
Bringing Your Smart Phone to Lunch & 50 Dumb Mistakes Great Managers Don't Make!

CORNERING SALES SUCCESS
How to Use the Intersection of Facts and Relationships to Increase Sales and Broaden Distribution

SEE YOU AT THE FINISH LINE
How To Outrun Ordinary and Achieve Extraordinary In Your Life

TEAM ENERGIZED!
50 Easy Ways To Fuel A Culture of Energy and Engagement At Your Company

There are many ways to run into a secure and comfortable retirement.

Doing nothing is not one of them!

About this Book

I have always found that marathon running is a great metaphor for many situations we find ourselves in during our lifetime. This is my eighth book, and I've used this analogy about sales, customer service, personal success, and management. These are all important topics, but now it's time to focus on the big picture—retirement.

I'm particularly fond of sharing a concept I call, *Surviving the Middle Miles.*

For every goal, every endeavor (including retirement planning), there is a point in the race where the excitement of the start has faded, but you can't yet imagine the sweet success of the Finish Line. Those are the middle miles. Many of us do everything we can to survive this part of the race. By Finish Line, I'm referring to the line that separates work from retirement! We survive the middle miles to reach retirement secure enough *to dote on our grandchildren if we like them or buy a flat screen TV if we don't!*

Soon, you'll arrive at the Starting Line of this book. After a few lines, you may think, "Is this guy going to talk about running the whole time?" Not at all. I promise. Although, in keeping with the running theme, there are 26.2 chapters. Naturally!

The. Race. Of. Your. Life! is designed to be a quick read. My intent is not for this book to be the be all, end all. There's plenty of information out there. My goal is to highlight important topics that you should think about when it comes to retirement planning. You'll find the chapters are in alphabetical order and each addresses a different topic. Feel free to open the book to any chapter and read that particular lesson. After you do that, I'd like you to ask yourself the following: Am I doing a good job? Have I considered this? Should I improve my plan?

The End of Each Chapter

Why does each chapter end the same way? You will notice that I end each chapter with the phrase, "That's just the way it works!" Actually, I have done this in all of my books. I want to emphasize that the principles I cover are straightforward and extremely effective when put into practice. Unfortunately, those lessons are often lost in the shuffle of other thoughts when we find ourselves in a situation in which we want to take our financial performance to the next level.

I also like to get the last word in . . .

So is this really THE. RACE. OF. YOUR. LIFE?

Well, I don't want to be melodramatic but I believe so. I used to run 5K (3.1 mile) road races. If the results weren't to my satisfaction (as they often weren't), I could easily enter a similar race the following weekend. Maybe even the following day! The importance of each individual race was muted. But what about the race to retirement? Is the race to retirement with enough cash and energy the race of YOUR lifetime?

I think you only get one chance to do what is necessary for SECURiMENT—a concept with which you will soon be familiar. My boys think this concept is silly, but they don't understand. They're young—with many years to go before this subject is relevant for them. I would rather they just say, thank you, for, I don't know, EVERYTHING, and go clean their rooms.

I didn't write this book for them. It's for you. I believe with all my heart that these pages will help you, so don't delay. Turn the page right now and start learning before it's too late!

This **IS** THE. RACE. OF. YOUR. LIFE!

That's just the way it works!

The. Race. Of. Your. Life!

How to reach retirement secure enough to dote on your grandkids (if you like them), or buy a flat screen TV (if you don't!)

Table of Contents

Introduction
Before the Race i
Race Instructions. vii
The Start—Have a Plan xi

The Race
Chapter 1: Avoid Unnecessary Taxation 1
Chapter 2: Be Real About Expenses. 5
Chapter 3: Buy A Pension (If You Don't Have One) 7
Chapter 4: Buy When Hamburgers Are Cheap. 11
Chapter 5: Control Your 401 (k) 13
Chapter 6: Convert While the Price Is Right 15
Chapter 7: Don't Be Greedy 17
Chapter 8: Don't Look Back 21
Chapter 9: Get Some Help 25
Chapter 10: Keep the Curtains Closed 29
Chapter 11: Know Your Risk Number 31
Chapter 12: Learn Wall Street's Tricks 35
Chapter 13: Leave Predictions to the Weather Forecaster. 39
Chapter 14: Manage the Max Drawdown 41
Chapter 15: Protect Your Principal 43
Chapter 16: Raise Some Cash 47
Chapter 17: Reduce Investment Volatility 49
Chapter 18: Run Your Own Race 51
Chapter 19: Save More 55
Chapter 20: Set Realistic Targets 59
Chapter 21: Simplify Your Plan 63
Chapter 22: Slay the Silent Retirement Killer. 67
Chapter 23: Stay On Course 69
Chapter 24: Stay Out of the Whackosphere! 71
Chapter 25: Take Some Risk. 75
Chapter 26: Write It Down 77
Chapter 26.2: The Final Straightaway 81

About the Pandemic 87
After the Finish Line 91

Before the Race

It felt like all I had worked for was slipping away.

It was October 2008. I was sitting at a hotel bar drinking a velvety Cabernet. I believe the bartender referred to it as Chateau Yesterday. Or maybe that was when it was made. Either way, it was the kind you'd offer to a wino and he'd say, No, I'm good."

I was somewhere near Atlanta—I think. Or maybe it was Atlantic City. Or Altoona. Or Albuquerque. I'm not sure. But here's what I *am* sure of: I was aggravated, I was depressed, and I felt all alone.

Never in my entire life had I felt so weak. So not in control. It seemed like everything I had worked for was slipping away. I have to tell you it was the darkest time of my life. If my wife had left me...and taken my pickup truck with her, we'd have had ourselves a pretty good country song!

To understand how I got there, we have to go back to my childhood. You see, I grew up in a liquor store.

No, it wasn't bad parenting, is was a family business. Our family owned a business called Sam's Wines & Spirits. You may remember Sam's—sort of an iconic brand back in the day. Now, of course, some of you may have been too drunk to remember Sam's—but you were our best customers!

Here's a little history. My Grandfather started Sam's in the 50's as a saloon. Not a bar—it was a saloon. There's a big difference. I was told that we had some interesting characters come in, most of whom are either dead now or in the Witness Protection Program.

Then shortly before I was born, my Grandfather turned Sam's into a liquor store. And as a kid, I was there all the time. While my friends were playing basketball, I was slinging cases of

Introduction

Budweiser and Dom Perignon. I learned very quickly that one was a little more expensive than the other. Yeah, if you drop a case of Dom Perignon, you'll learn quickly, too.

This may explain why I could never figure out how to dribble a basketball. When I went one way, the ball went the other way... But if there had ever been a need to stack basketballs, or chill basketballs, or do inventory of basketballs, well, I would have had my friends beat, hands down.

Fast forward through my high school years, my college years, and I became a CPA because I wanted a fast paced, exciting career... After a few years of doing that, my Dad asked me to join the family business. He wanted me to help him gain some financial control over a growing business.

So, I left behind the *scintillating* world of public accounting and entered the family business fulltime. I know, I know, you're all thinking, "Darryl, no way! You left the exciting world of public accounting behind for the family business? The glitz, the glamour, the ledger paper?" Yep, I did just that.

I was 24-years-old. And for the next 17 years, I was strapped into a roller coaster, that just kept going and going and going and never stopped. And two things happened: I continued to grow *in* the business. And as I continued to grow in the business, I continued to grow the actual business itself.

I took over the leadership in my early 30's; poured every ounce of my heart and soul into that business. We grew to new heights and when the time seemed right, I drove the sale of the business.

That business was everything I had—emotionally and financially. It was my identity. I was Sam's and Sam's was me. That sounds like something from a bad Dr. Seuss book. Sadly, the Grinch was about to take my money.

The year was 2007! I was 41 years of age. Too old to win one of those "Young Entrepreneur" Awards and too young for my

AARP card. But despite everything else, after the sale I was doing ok financially. Not that I had Bill Gates's wealth per se, but it was my financial high-water mark. Now, at this point, I wish I could share some revolutionary story of turning a small pot into a big one—but I can't. Of my assets growing—nope, my assets were going.

You see, I received terrible (life-altering) financial guidance. Nobody asked me the hard questions. How long it would take to start a new business? How much I was spending? What kind of big expenditures were upcoming—like a giant tax bill? Nobody took stock of where the markets were. Were we near the top? Could a correction be coming? Should we wait a little? So, I was not doing anything close to the right thing with my money. Instead, everything was immediately invested. The only question asked was—who do I send the invoice to?

Let me say this again—and try not to throw up a little in my mouth when I say it—everything—everything was immediately invested. Sure, I could have paid more attention. Suffice it to say, selling the business was an emotional process. My head was not in the right place.

You know the song, "My Way" by Frank Sinatra? There's a line in there, "Regrets. I've had a few. But then again, too few to mention." Well, this is definitely something I regret and definitely something I want to mention, and need to mention, and is the catalyst for the entire reason I'm where I am today. Because I don't want any of you to ever go through what I went through.

Here's a silly question: remember what happened in 2007?

When I share this story with my audiences, I ask people to raise their hands if they look back at those years fondly. Recently a guy enthusiastically raised his hand. Turns out he was a bankruptcy attorney... Me, not so fond memories. As the markets were falling and falling and falling, I was selling and selling and selling. It's October and I'm traveling the country trying to build a beverage consulting business (hence) somewhere outside of Atlanta or Altoona or wherever), and my

Introduction

investments are tanking. Every day lower. All the while, I'm selling stock to pay my bills. I've never felt so weak. (When you sell into weakness, it never comes back!)

It should have been a happy time. I should have been making a killing. And now the markets were killing me. But I don't give up easily. Never have. So I fought back. There must be a better way to protect money I thought. There must be a better way to grow money. To save money on taxes. Better investments. Better tools. Better strategy. A better approach.

I immersed myself in learning how to make better financial decisions. During the day I helped individuals and companies sell wine hopefully a bit more elegant than the Chateau I was drinking yesterday in the hotel bar. At night I studied. I figured this can't be rocket science. And it wasn't. It was "Financial Science." And I learned how it worked. How to take control. How to flex my financial muscle.

I use this image to illustrate strength. A visual reminder for you the reader, but also to remind me that I will never operate with weakness ever again. Incidentally, some people accuse me of not looking like this in real life. They are correct – I have no tattoos!

I began operating from a position of strength and over time the cloud lifted. It wasn't immediate, but the weakness dissipated.

Anyway, before long, I left the beverage industry behind. Because from the depths of despair, I had found something I was even *more* passionate about. I created a business (and a concept) which will change how you view money. Certainly, how you view this stage of your life. Your eyesight may be starting to decline, but this view I'm going to share with you will have you seeing your money with 20/20 vision. And as we go into the year 2020, what better time to change your view of money.

The skills I used to create financial strength form the basis of a concept called SECURiMENT. I know, it's a weird word. It sounds like something that would hold your dentures in. SECURiMENT. But, trust me, it will be far more important than something having to do with your teeth. SECURiMENT will hold your future in place. Then you can worry about your teeth!

You will become infinitely familiar with SECURiMENT by reading this book.

Simply: Experience is much less costly, when you let someone else pay for it! (YOU ARE WELCOME!)

By the way, can this happen to your money? What is one advantage that I had in my story that you don't have?

Yes, you got it. I was 41. Too old for snapchat, and yes, thankfully, too young to worry about my teeth falling out. I had time. If you're reading this book, I'm guessing you're older than I was back in those days.

Are you worried about making poor decisions and destroying what you've worked for?

Not on my watch!

Introduction

My goal is to help you operate from a position of strength. To guide you to your vision of SECURiMENT, in such a way that you're comfortable taking control of your financial future! I help people feel as good about their future as I feel about mine.

As I will share throughout this book. This is the race of your life and you only get one chance to get it right. If you have read this far—congratulations! You have made it to the start line. You've chosen to toe the line, which puts you in better shape than most others. Make sure your shoes are laced because we're about to get started!

Clearly, I can't see the future because I'm not a future teller but I can see the following: The SECURiMENT approach will help you see your future more clearly. 20/20 vision if you will, which is nice heading into the year 2020!

Race Instructions

I've heard it said that if you can't explain a concept in one sentence...it's too complicated! Touché! I'll try to keep this brief, but I do need one *short* chapter to shed some light on the SECURiMENT concept.

I define SECURiMENT as peace of mind in retirement. Not extraordinary riches, but immense wealth. Happiness and the permission and resources to enjoy your second act. I created the SECURiMENT concept to help you reduce worry, crush anxiety and kick your financial stress to the curb. I want you to be in a position to dote on your grandkids if you like them or buy a wide-screen TV if you don't.

There are two non-negotiable steps to SECURiMENT.

First, you must be able to visualize—in extraordinary detail - what peace-of-mind means to you. My vision of SECURiMENT is irrelevant. Peace of mind is vague, which is why YOUR vision of this feeling must be developed. For example, if your goal is to drive a Winnebago across the country, I want you to visualize the license plate. And the upholstery. Visualize who you're with, where you're going and how often you're hitting the open road. Want the best results? Write it all down. Does this *drive* the point home? (See what I did there? Never mind!) Here's a quick example from my detailed SECURiMENT vision.

I'd like to attend more Cubs games in retirement. And when I do, Jill and I are going to stay in the city the night before. Maybe on Michigan avenue, maybe in that fancy, new Cubs hotel by Wrigley. See, I abhor the process of actually getting to the game! Going from Deerfield to Wrigley almost guarantees that I won't go. The point is we have taken our thinking to the next level and consequently, that extra detail helps motivate us to plan appropriately.

So that's step one and if you aren't willing to visualize in this manner, please don't even bother with step two. I know that seems harsh but without step one, you won't be motivated

Introduction

enough to take the process seriously. The status quo will keep you exactly where you are!

Make sure to read the chapter titled "The Final Straightaway" for more detail on Step One.

Second, you must aim for the bullseye in the middle of the SECURiMENT wheel.

As you know, SECURiMENT lies at the intersection of three critical variables.

1) Income Planning—creating multiple streams of monthly income
2) Investment Volatility Management—reducing the range of investment returns and protecting your nest egg
3) Cash Efficiency—make strong decisions about social security, long term care, taxes, etc.

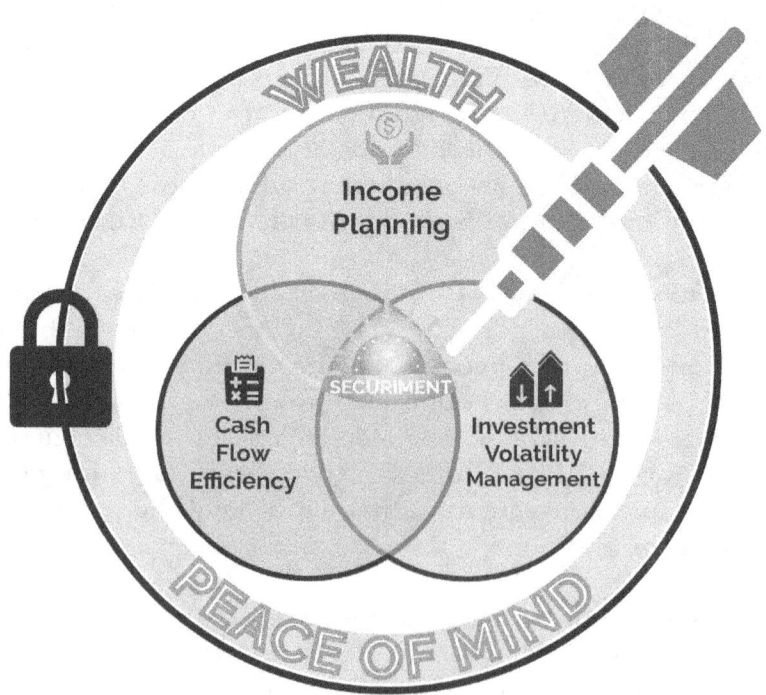

Race Instructions

For there to be success, you must aim at the bullseye.

Let's use the marathon as an example. For there to be success on marathon day, everything has to go right. Sufficient rest, ample nutrition, the right pace. Proper hydration is vital as is having friends and family along the route. Don't forget proper footwear. You can't pick and choose among these variables as it doesn't work that way. Months of rigorous training but forgetting to eat during the race will sap your energy long before the finish line. Having enough rest but wearing a brand-spanking new pair of running shoes will make excruciating blisters the day's lasting memory!

Ignoring multiple variables, in lieu of just one area...will greatly reduce your chances for SECURiMENT! You must aim at the center. That's where you have the best chance at success.

Introduction

One more point: See the lock on the left of the SECURiMENT wheel a few pages ago? The lock had two meanings.

First, you must take action to unlock the SECURiMENT Wheel. The key, if you will, is taking action. SECURiMENT doesn't just happen because you want it to. It takes work.

Second, and this is a biggie, once you have taken action to create SECURiMENT, it is extraordinarily difficult to lose it. You're locked in; almost held captive like a hostage. Ok, that came out wrong! You know what I mean—I hope. Once plans are made, your future will be more certain. You can relax, which is the whole idea!

Look, let's be candid about this. You and me: we ain't getting any younger. As we age, we are going to lose some of the cognitive ability we need to make good financial decisions. That's why doing something NOW is so critical. Create SECURiMENT before it's too late!

You'll be happy you did.

That's just the way it works!

The Start—Have a Plan

When I was 12 years old, my dad came home from work and made a huge announcement. It was time for him to quit smoking and get in shape. I later found out that it was actually my mom's suggestion that he quit smoking and get in shape. So, the following evening, my dad and I ran, walked, trudged, and maybe even crawled a bit during our two-mile journey to one of the most amazing places you can go during the summer.

Yep, the local Dairy Queen. We ordered hot fudge sundaes and called mom for a ride home. It was her idea after all...

The next year as a spry 13-year-old, I became one of the youngest finishers in Chicago Marathon history. In high school, I ran track and cross country. You know, the glamour sports...

(That's a joke. Everyone knows the glamour sports are lacrosse and field hockey.)

Anyway, after four years of college where the only running I did was to Domino's for pizza and just starting a career, it was time to get back in shape. I was living near Chicago's amazing lakefront, so each day after work I'd head to the running path alongside it and work up a sweat. In no time, the pounds fell off and my pace quickened. I started to have crazy thoughts.

Should I run a marathon again? Not just any marathon, but the most important one of them all – the Boston Marathon. For those who spend their time observing more mainstream (normal) sports, the Boston Marathon is unique because it's virtually the only marathon besides ones associated with the Olympics that you must run a certain time to qualify for. They don't let just anyone Boston.

So, I had a goal and thought it would be a piece of cake. After all, I ran in high school, right? Picture me back then with hair blowing in the wind . . . female classmates sighing with admiration as I run by them. The hair part - most people can imagine. But the girls admiring me part, nobody ever believes!

Introduction

At any rate, I trained hard. I was strong, fit, and fast. "Just do it," I told myself, as I tightly laced up my Nike running shoes.

It was time!

When the gun went off, I took off like I was running the 100-yard dash. Like the finish line was right around the corner. Pace yourself - for some reason, I didn't get that memo. By six miles in, I was hurting. Ten miles, I was really struggling. Twelve miles, I was walking; and you guessed it, at 14 miles, I was looking for a taxi. (For you younger readers, Uber didn't exist yet!)

Well, this certainly wasn't how this day was supposed to go. I tried to call my friends and family from a payphone, but nobody answered. (This is my last shout out to the younger demographic. Payphones were big boxes that you could use to call people. They are basically extinct now!)

Why aren't they answering? They were all at the Finish Line wondering what happened to me. I never got to see their signs of encouragement: "Go Darryl!", "You can do it, Darryl!", and my personal favorite – "Don't die, Darryl!"

While my friends and family were waiting for me at the Finish Line, I was finishing a ham and cheese omelet. It was the only thing I finished that day. Now, here is the important part to remember. As I devoured that delicious breakfast (14 miles can make you hungry), I tried to make sense of what happened. It occurred to me that there must be a lesson from the humiliation I was now suffering through.

The lesson was maybe I should've tried a half-marathon!

No, not that lesson, a better one for those of you who are still reading, based upon my unfortunate day. Here it is. It's the first of many in this book. You must have a plan because goals without plans are just daydreams. They don't motivate you. They're not actionable. They don't work. I thought I could simply pin an entry number on my shirt and go. I would have no problem whatsoever running a time in Chicago that so many weren't even capable of. Then, I could head to Beantown for an even greater victory. Not a chance. Oh, I trained all right, but I lacked a coordinated plan for traversing the entire marathon course.

So, that's one of my favorite stories. But let's talk about you, now. Do you have a plan for what you want to get done today? What you are going to do at work? Most importantly, do you have a retirement plan? Do you know how you are going to achieve your retirement goals? You have goals, don't you? Everybody thinks about the future: Travel, read, paint, spoil the grandkids. However, without a solid plan to have enough dough to live life on your terms and at your pace, it's just a daydream.

That's why I wrote this book. I want you to think about your journey to retirement.

Here's another running analogy to visualize.

If you stand and watch runners at the 25-mile mark of most marathons, it may seem like you're watching the walk of the living dead. Many participants are walking and/or limping and seem to be talking to themselves. They move with a bit of a shuffle. Their feet don't leave the ground in any measurable way. They're exhausted and wear an uncomfortable (almost disoriented) look on their faces. Perhaps from exhaustion caused by the 25 miles of pounding or even from the discomfort caused by chafing, which, as a friend once told me, "There is no good kind of chafing . . . ."

At this point, running seems so painful for so many, but not all. There are runners who pass by smiling, waving, and interacting with the crowd. They're ecstatic. After all, there is just one measly mile to go. The last mile seems small when compared to the ground they've already covered. These warriors make it seem like the race has only just begun. Their energy seems boundless. They're the ones who will preen for the camera when they cross the Finish Line. Happy. Content.

Introduction

Satisfied. They'll be smiling and their photos will go viral. They did it on their own terms; at their own pace.

Lessons learned by the divergence of euphoria and agony of "da feet" while attempting the grueling marathon distance have similarities for those hoping for a secure and comfortable retirement.

Think about it this way. You can either cross the Finish Line that separates work from retirement with jubilance and happiness or with snot covering your face AND your clothes rubbing you in uncomfortable places. (I had to go there. They say a picture paints a thousand words.) But seriously, as you make one of life's greatest transitions, you can either feel jubilation and excitement or fear and despair. Much of it will be determined by how seriously you take the exercise of creating a financial plan for retirement.

Having done marathons where I'm either suffering or smiling as I run that last mile, I know with certainty that runners who complete a marathon with relative ease, have a plan for doing so. The same can be said for the employee who retires into a situation that is comfortable and secure.

Forbes stated:

> *"It's one thing not to have a financial plan when you're 25. At that point, your financial plan is to simply save as much as you can. It's completely different when you're 55.*
>
> *"The closer you are to retirement, the more you need a financial plan. Without one, you can't know if you're on track. And if you don't know where you stand, you're just throwing money at your investment account. That's not the worst thing you can do, but you can do better.*
>
> *"Your financial plan doesn't need to be a massive 200-page document. It just needs to identify where you are today, where you want to be, and how you will bridge the gap. The more specific you get the better, but even a basic idea will put you ahead of almost everyone."*

How do you want to feel at your retirement party? I can promise you that the champagne is going to be much sweeter if you're smiling at the end of the race.

That's just the way it works!

Chapter 1
Avoid Unnecessary Taxation

Do you ever get the sense that you're being forced to take more and more risk to earn a reasonable rate of return on your low-risk investments? If you do, you're not alone.

I read recently that savers must take *four times more risk* these days than they had to in 1985 to make a measly 5% return on their investments. Wow, that's a bunch of risk to take for a small amount of return. Part of this is the result of the risk-free rate of return continuing to be so low. As you know, the risk-free rate of return is a theoretical rate of return of an investment with zero risk. As our parents headed towards retirement many years ago, the risk-free rate was much higher. Currently, even though the Federal Reserve has raised interest rates a bit recently, rates are still extremely low. In what seems like a cruel twist of fate, every April taxpayers must give a share of their paltry returns to the Internal Revenue Service.

> *Do you want to keep the tiny amounts of interest you're currently earning in your checking, savings, and money market investments?*

If you're vigorously shaking your head up and down and muttering "YES," then keep reading. The sad reality is that many savers are unintentionally sabotaging their portfolios by having too much money in taxable accounts.

The Three Buckets Analogy
Let's assume there are three types of accounts (or buckets) where all your money goes.

> 1) Taxable Bucket: Earnings are taxable each year (Savings accounts, checking accounts, traditional brokerage accounts, etc.)

2) Tax-Deferred Bucket: Money is taxable when you take it out (401(k) accounts, IRAs, etc.)

3) Tax-Free Bucket: Money is no longer on IRS's radar (Roth accounts, certain types of carefully created cash-value life insurance policies.)

Financial experts don't agree on much. However, one concept with uniform consensus is that you should always have at least six months of income on hand in the taxable bucket for life's unexpected expenses and emergencies. Yet in spite of the agreement of the experts, many people have much more in their taxable bucket than is necessary. Money in these accounts is often in low-interest investments such as savings, money markets, conservative bonds, etc. Ignoring the scenario of paying too much tax for a moment, remember that inflation will reduce your purchasing power over time at ultra-low rates of return.

You may be thinking, "Ok, then what can I do?"

You could invest in a Roth IRA. Those who have work wages, but don't make too much money are eligible. It makes great sense to contribute to a Roth IRA. There are several reasons to love Roth accounts.

The tax-free nature of Roth accounts is a plus. Once money is placed in a Roth account, as long as laws stay the same, it will never be taxed again. Further, Roth accounts don't figure into the calculation for Provisional Income, which determines whether or not your Social Security gets taxed. (Hint: You don't want your social security taxed.)

By keeping more than you need in your taxable bucket, you are ultimately paying a (figurative) penalty.

Imagine for a moment that you have $100K in a money market account. Even if you are only earning 1% or something similarly appalling, you're going to pay tax on that interest each year. This adds insult to injury. If rates rise, you'll earn more interest, but you'll also pay more tax.

So start moving some of that money into the tax-free bucket. Of course, there are limits to who can make a Roth contribution because a Roth account is a product for Main Street, not Wall Street. Unfortunately, if you earn too much, Roth accounts won't be an option for you. However, a Roth IRA allows cases where you can contribute for a non-working spouse and there are provisions that let you contribute more as you get older.

The bottom line is that Roth accounts should definitely be part of your race plan!

That's just the way it works!

Chapter 2
Be Real About Expenses

The fact that many future retirees proclaim that their living expenses will be lower in retirement is an interesting phenomenon to me. They talk about fewer dry cleaning bills, less wear and tear on their vehicles because they won't have to drive to and from work. But they ignore the "new" expenses that might come their way. (Especially health care costs as you age!)

It's not just the normal stuff, but the unforeseen expenses that can ruin retirement. Typically, retirees' new spending patterns could include the following:

1) Travel
2) New hobbies
3) Doting on grandchildren!

Traveling to exotic destinations, maybe even with your family in tow, are wonderful ways to spend your retirement years. But these activities are optional. What about stuff that's beyond your control? If you live in Illinois, you may pay high property taxes that rise year after year because of state budget problems. What about your home? You may *finally* be free of a mortgage, but you're likely to incur higher home maintenance costs. The older your property, the more likely you'll have to have the local repairmen on speed dial.

I often wonder how come people don't get real about expenses?

My experience is that it's easier to sweep this subject under the nearest rug. Rate of return and asset diversification are not emotional topics. But, living life comfortably (on your terms) is a topic loaded with emotion, and I find it's more difficult to consider. But the issue still exists: Do expenses really go down during retirement?

Here is my professional answer: Maybe!

Whatever the case, you'll be better off using a higher expense figure in your retirement calculations, rather than the lower numbers that might look better on the calculator. Using a more conservative figure will provide more flexibility in later years because you'll spend less of your nest egg. You may not live life *exactly* in a manner that pleases you, but the downside of outliving your money will be much less likely.

The truth is that expenses may change in retirement, but it's less accurate to suggest that they will be lower.

Future retirees who do a thorough analysis about retirement expenses are more informed and more likely to spend accordingly. Many have a goal of spending less money in retirement, but studies suggest that this is not the case. One study (McKinsey) reported that *32% of retirees expected to reduce their expenses, yet only 10% did.*

J.P. Morgan also found the following:

> *"For lower-income households, there's less ability to reduce spending, since a larger percentage of their income is going to essentials," says Katherine Roy, chief retirement strategist at J.P. Morgan, who led the study by her bank. "Wealthier households have more discretionary income, so it's easier to trim in retirement."*

I'd like to share a final thought with you. My purpose isn't to scare you and cause you to go live in a hole somewhere where your credit cards don't work. I don't even want my boys (and Jill) to go somewhere where my credit cards don't work.

But there are many elements that go into a comprehensive retirement plan. Level of savings, assumed rates of return, years to retirement, etc. I feel that people are too casual when it comes to this part of their plan. I think it's because many don't want to confront the possibility that they may not live out their years in a manner that's consistent or preferable to them.

That's just the way it works.

Chapter 3
Buy A Pension (If You Don't Have One)

Do you ever notice who the happiest retirees are? The people with guaranteed pensions, that's who!

They're the ones with a little extra pep in their step. They seem just a bit happier.

They're the teachers, firefighters, and those fortunate enough to have cash deposited directly into their bank accounts—like clockwork—every month when their careers end.

Month after month in retirement—money they can't outlive.

This used to be the norm for most of America. After giving blood, sweat, and even some tears for 30 years or so, many retirees would receive monthly income. It was known as a defined benefit pension plan.

Most retirees knew it as peace of mind, even if they didn't call it that.

According to the Bureau of Labor Statistics, just 13% of Americans currently have a defined benefit pension plan, as compared to 76% in the mid-1980s.

Back then, there were fewer decisions for retirees. Life was simpler with a check in the mailbox every month. Some called it "mailbox money."

Maybe today it would be called a *dependable deposit*. Something you could count on. Not in the mailbox, but rather a transfer directly into your checking account. You wouldn't even have to leave the house. Keep your pajamas on all day!

Everything changed in the late seventies when a benefits consultant named Ted Benna discovered a little-known part

The. Race. Of. Your. Life!

of the tax code that gave companies a tax break for allowing employees to save some money on the side.

The 401(k) was born.

It took off. Companies ran with it because it was cheaper. The great shift began. The burden for retirement began to be transferred or shifted from the employer to the employee. What's not to love—if you were the employer. It was significantly cheaper. For the employee, the benefits weren't as clear. The plans could be confusing. Costly.

I read somewhere that 92% of Americans have no clue what costs they pay within their 401(k) plans. Some plans have too many choices for investing money. Others? Not enough choices.

When pensions were prevalent, **income was all that mattered**. Mailbox money didn't come from selling your investments. Mailbox money didn't require you to manage the ups and downs in the market. It wasn't based on projected-maybe-down-the-road assumptions.

The 401(k) was supposed to be a savings plan. Incidental. Not a retirement plan but a way to save a few dollars. Incidentally, remember Ted Benna, the creator of the 401(k) concept? He hates it. Calls it a monster and says it has gone awry.

Now, millions of Americans have their retirement dreams riding on a misunderstanding that their 401(k)s and IRAs are retirement plans. They're not.

The American Society of Pension Professionals & Actuaries says this about the 401(k) plan:
> *"The great lie is that the 401(k) was capable of replacing the old system of pensions!"*

These days, people are left to their own devices.

The pension was a reliable way to put dollars in your checking account. Now, people are forced to make complex financial decisions as they age. It's a recipe for disaster. Do you want to make complex financial decisions as you age?

If you don't have a pension, buy one.

Build a financial plan that can withstand the gauntlet of risks that you'll face over the remainder of your life. Buy guaranteed income for life.

Guaranteed income for life is like a personal "pension plan." It's a way to receive periodic payments for as long as you live. The income stream may be level or increased annually to hedge against inflation. Income can be designed to last for a minimum number of years or paid throughout the life span of one person or the life spans of two people (known as joint income).

With guaranteed income, you are effectively shifting the burden of creating pension-like income to an entity better equipped to handle such risk. In retirement, your (hopefully) multiple guaranteed streams of income should combine to be as close to your spending needs as possible. Sometimes you can't get to 100%, but that should always be the goal.

The key to SECURiMENT is not the next bull or bear market. Mailbox money and dependable deposits don't come from following the next great stock picker. They come from converting a part of your IRA/401(k) to a stream of income. Like a money tree, if you will! Unfortunately, if you aren't lucky enough to have a beefy pension plan, you must buy one.

That's just the way it works!

Chapter 4
Buy When Hamburgers Are Cheap

Warren Buffet is one of the most respected stock investors in history. Known as the *Oracle of Omaha*, he is an investor and philanthropist and one of the wealthiest people in the United States. His investing style and success have been the subject of numerous articles and books. His quotes are legendary. But there is one quote in particular that guides my own investing style:

> "To refer to a personal taste of mine, I'm going to buy hamburgers the rest of my life. When hamburgers go down in price, we sing the 'Hallelujah Chorus' in the Buffett household. When hamburgers go up in price, we weep. For most people, it's the same with everything in life they will be buying - except stocks. When stocks go down and you can get more for your money, people don't like them anymore."

Let's think about this for a moment. There's a reason why so many of us shop at Costco, which made $118 billion in sales in 2016. It's because we all like a good deal. Toilet paper, bottled water, Kellogg's Mini-Wheats - you name it. We get it all at Costco. And this may shock you, but my dress shirts aren't from Italy, unless Costco makes its Kirkland brand where pizza originated! But Buffet is right about hamburgers and stocks. Investors are an emotional breed. They don't want to be left behind. They chase returns, and instead of buying stocks when valuations are cheap, they buy stocks at inflated values.

Whether stocks are cheap or expensive is typically determined by the price-earnings (P/E) ratio. Per John Mauldin's newsletter, Thoughts From The Frontline:

> "If your stock price is $10 and your current earnings per share is $2, then your stock price is trading at a P/E of 5 (or simply $10 divided by $2 equals 5). It is simply a metric to see if your 'hamburger' is pricey or cheap."

At a P/E of 5, the hamburger may be a bargain! But what if the burger is priced at 48, with the same earnings of $2 dollars per share? Now, the burger is expensive with a P/E of 24. If the average P/E for the S&P 500 for the last 52 years was 17, then our burger better taste pretty darn good because it's mighty pricey.

And that's where we find ourselves - mired in a very expensive market. The $64,000 question is: What does this tell us about returns going forward?

Ned Davis Research has studied price data from 1926 to 2018. It has divided P/E ratios into 5 categories from the cheapest 20 percent to the most expensive 20 percent. Then, they looked at forward 10-year returns by taking each month-end P/E and calculating the subsequent 10-year annualized S&P return. From the *Thoughts From The Frontline* newsletter:

> "With a current median P/E for the S&P of 24, we find ourselves firmly in quintile 5. That tells us to expect low returns over the coming 10 years. Though it appears that most investors are expecting 10% from equities, history tells us that the market as a whole (based on where we are today) will have a hard time growing much faster than our country's GDP does."

What does all this mean? Unless this time is different (and it's not), hamburgers are expensive. For now, it's time to play defense and think differently about your portfolio. Raise some cash because it would certainly be nice to have some money when burgers go on sale!

That's just the way it works!

Chapter 5
Control Your 401(k)

When at workshops, I am routinely asked: What is an in-service distribution and should I do one? Investopedia defines this for us.

> *An In-Service Distribution is a withdrawal made from a qualified plan account before the holder experiences a triggering event. A triggering event, such as reaching a certain age, or leaving an employer, is often needed to be able to withdraw funds from a plan, such as a 401(k).*

An in-service distribution is relevant when the account holder still works at the company where the account is held. Some plans allow this distribution. However, there is no requirement that a retirement plan permit in-service distributions.

For those of you who have either reached age 59 1/2 or have a plan that allows you to do an in-service distribution, this chapter is for you! Not sure if your plan offers such distributions? Review your plan document or speak to your retirement plan administrator.

Generally, I recommend in-service distributions if possible. Here's why:

Improved diversification
Many 401(k) plans have limited investment options and by rolling your money into an Individual Retirement Account (IRA), you may have more investment choices.

Greater control
As the owner of the IRA, you can determine which investments to include and the timing of making investments, which may be restricted inside of an employer retirement account (401(k)). This is unfortunate, but never trust that your employer will take care of your retirement or that they provided the best retirement plan possible. Most often, the retirement plan you have was never meant to be the best, merely, the cheapest.

Increased beneficiary options
Typically, the options available for non-spouse beneficiaries of an IRA are more liberal than options available to a non-spouse beneficiary inside an employer retirement plan.

Professional management
It is usually much easier to find a professional money manager for an IRA. The limited options available inside an employer plan makes it more difficult for a professional manager to provide adequate diversification or risk avoidance. Most people need this help because, sadly, investors are typically quite bad at, well, investing. (Google the term Dalbar; you'll see that the average stock fund does better than the average investor.)

Lower costs and transparency
Escape a plan that has high expenses. Some plans have annual fees that are way above average. If you're stuck in one, you can reduce costs by rolling your 401(k) money into an IRA with a lower-cost fund company. (Note: According to a 2010 study conducted by Woelfel Research, Inc., 71% of people think they pay no fees in their company sponsored plans, which is kind ridiculous because financial firms don't do anything for free!)

As with anything else, you should check with a tax professional if you're considering an in-service distribution. An in-service rollover from your employer's plan into an individual retirement account can be a useful option in the right circumstances, but it is not for everyone. **If done improperly, it can become a taxable transaction.** Also, there is a 60-day window for account holders to move their money into an IRA after withdrawing it from their 401(k). This can be accomplished either by a direct transfer from your 401(k) plan to the IRA or by having the money sent to your bank account for deposit into your IRA. The simplest, easiest, and best way is via a direct transfer, and your plan administrator will have the necessary forms.

That's just the way it works!

Chapter 6
Convert While the Price Is Right

Do you know the television game show called, *The Price Is Right*? On this iconic show, which is still running strong after first debuting in 1956, the host encourages contestants to guess the price of a car, appliance or vacation of their dreams. The contestant who is closest to the actual price, wins the prize. But for many contestants, the price is nowhere near right, which makes for some good laughs!

I may not know how much a luxury camper costs, but I do know a place where the *price is most certainly right*. The price of our historically low tax rates. Yet when I speak to groups and I poll attendees to gauge their view on current rates, I'm often dumbfounded by their answers: "Taxes are so high", "Taxes are suffocating me!" or "They can't go any higher!"

Newsflash: Tax rates are extraordinarily low. You might say they are on sale! Today, the highest marginal tax bracket is 37%. But in 1944, the highest marginal tax rate was 94%. In the 1970s, the highest rate was 70%. We have had numerous eras in history where tax rates were significantly higher than they are today.

The reason why I'm sharing this history lesson is to encourage you to consider Roth conversions. In one of the quirks of the U.S. Tax Code, you are perfectly welcome to convert parts of your IRA to a Roth account at any time. Roth conversions are great because, once your funds are in a Roth account, they are no longer subject to taxation. Further, and this is beyond the scope of this book, Roth money doesn't figure in the calculation that determines if your social security will be taxed. Like a diet full of fruits & vegetables, Roth accounts are good for you! But there is a catch! You must pay taxes in the year of the conversion. It seems that tax rates will likely be higher in the future. Maybe not 94%, like after WWII, but higher than today's discount rates. This makes conversions appealing!

Many factors could cause an increase in taxes. According to NationalPriorities.org, in 2016, the four biggest expense categories - Medicare, Social Security, Medicaid, and interest payments on the national debt - consumed 66 cents of every dollar. In 2020, these same categories ate up 92 cents of every dollar of revenue. This leaves every other government agency to fight over just eight cents on the dollar.

David Walker is perhaps the most knowledgeable person in the country when it comes to this situation. He is a former Comptroller General for the United States. The CPA of the USA - if you will. (Incidentally, Mr. Walker is a member of the CPA Hall of Fame. I am also a CPA, but, strangely, they have not called me yet . . .) Anyway, these are his profound words:

> "Regardless of what politicians tell you, any additional accumulations of debt are, absent dramatic reductions in the size and role of government are basically deferred tax increases...Unless we get our fiscal house in order, there's simply no other way to handle our ever-mounting debt burdens except by doubling taxes over time."

Unfortunately, I agree. It's a math problem. Either taxes go up or spending decreases. But, in the end, it will be a combination of the two. And I know as I type this in Spring 2021, the subject of tax policy is still front and center. I fear that current congressional leadership will pay for those reductions in revenue on the backs of middle-income folks like you and me. Changing Medicare or tinkering with Social Security in a way that saves the government money but hurts many Americans when they need the help the most.

If you have invested heavily in tax-deferred accounts like 401(k)s and IRAs, and unless you can accurately predict what taxes rates will look like in the future, you don't know how much money you have. That makes it hard to plan for retirement. Today, the price is right for Roth conversions.

That's just the way it works!

Chapter 7
Don't Be Greedy

We had a day of reckoning recently in the Rosen household.

Frankly, it was a long time coming, and I had resisted. I didn't want to go there. I didn't want to stir the pot in such a dramatic way, but finally, I put my foot down and said, "No more!"

I told the boys they could no longer use my Starbucks card. I know, it's terrible, but before you call the authorities, let me explain.

At the time of this writing, Josh is 26 and gainfully employed as an airline pilot. He still asks me to pay for everything, but I think he's just trying to push my buttons. It's working.

Danny is 23. He has a great job and has plenty of money for Starbucks. Ben, 18, makes money selling IOS programs in the app store.

I didn't cut their privileges because of money. Rather, it was the principle.

See, they wouldn't pay for any of their multiple trips per day to Starbucks, nor would they buy me anything when they went.

"We're saving," they would say. All the while, I'm thinking "Me too! I'm saving for retirement." And through it all, I saw something I didn't like—*greed*.

If only they had used their own funds here and there, perhaps I would have felt differently. But I believed they were being greedy, and it upset me.

So, I put my foot down. (**Postscript**: They're using the Keurig now, which I bought, so go figure!)

Unfortunately, in my role as a retirement strategist, I run into greed a fair bit.

From my friends at realinvestmentadvice.com:

> *"Greed causes investors to lose more money investing than any other emotion.*
>
> *The human emotion of 'greed' leads to 'confirmation bias where individuals become blinded to contrary evidence leading them to overstay their welcome.*
>
> *Individuals regularly fall prey to the notion that if they 'sell' a position to realize a 'profit' that they may be 'missing out' on further gains. This mentality has a long and depressing history of turning unrealized gains into realized losses as the investment eventually plummets back to earth.*
>
> *It is important to remember that the primary tenant of investing is to 'buy low' and 'sell high.' While this seems completely logical, it is emotionally impossible to achieve. It is 'greed' that keeps us from selling high, and 'fear' that keeps us from buying low. In the end, we are only left with poor results."*

All of this takes on added importance as retirement nears.

So, here are a few nuggets of guidance that you can take right to the nearest coffee shop.

- The markets are still at historically high levels. They have been for a while. There is far greater risk on the downside than there is opportunity for gains on the upside.

- Set a floor on some of your retirement money. That is, if you're 60 years of age, for example, protect 60% of your principal so that this money can never be any lower in value than it is today. As you move along in retirement, continue to raise the floor on your assets.

- Don't succumb to the *fear of missing out* (words that have ruined many of the best-laid retirement plans).

With proper planning and a bit of smarts when it comes to knowing when *good enough is good enough*, you just may have enough money for Starbucks in your golden years. (If you see the boys there, make sure they're using their own cards!)

That's just the way it works!

Chapter 8
Don't Look Back

"It's not where you've been; it's where you're going."

My dad spoke those words to me nearly 35 years ago, and the lesson has stuck with me ever since.

Here's the story and why it matters for you.

It was 1984, and I had just spent my freshman year of college bouncing around the Midwest like a ping-pong ball. Because I was an underachiever in high school, my college choices were limited.

Three schools accepted me. None were of interest to me.

I chose The University of Iowa, but I never wanted to go there. Never even visited the campus. Although I looked stunning in their school colors, my world was hundreds of miles away.

See, my twin sister and three best friends in high school all left the same day for Indiana University. On top of that, Jill, my girlfriend (now my wife of 28 years), was still a senior in high school.

At Iowa, I was stuck in temporary housing in the legendary dormitory known as The Burge. Some of the guys probably loved it. It was a big party scene. A bunch of newly free-from-their-parents freshmen living in bunk beds. Girls, beer, fun—what else could you ask for?

I hadn't asked for that.

(I know I seem like the life of the party now [*kidding*], but back then I was more reserved. Beer bongs were not my thing!)

I hated Iowa. (Not the whole state; just the University.)

Calls to my sister at Indiana didn't help. (Good thing there was no Facebook then. At least I couldn't see what I was missing!)

So, one day after a few weeks, I called my dad. (My mom was sick at the time. She passed away the next year.)

"Dad, I don't like it here," I said.

He asked me to give it more time. He told me it would get better. We actually spoke for more than three minutes, which was very rare.

I hung up and began packing.

I waited about an hour and called him again.

"Dad, I don't like it here."

This time, he implored me to resist doing anything rash.

So I heeded his advice, got in the car and drove home. The moral of the story is to never let a freshman have a car at school. (Incidentally, I left a three-speed bicycle on campus. Maybe you could pick it up if you happen to visit Iowa City?)

Anyway, the whole thing was absolutely devastating. I didn't know what to do. Go back? Go somewhere else? Become a professional basket weaver?

You should have seen Jill's parents. Their combined look spoke a thousand, sad words: "What's this loser doing back in town?"

The next day, I enrolled at DePaul University. They must have been hurting for students. My second semester was spent at Eastern Illinois University, where I knew some guys who were running track. I just wanted to get away.

After earning wonderful grades that year, I was accepted into Indiana University for my sophomore year, and the rest is history. I studied accounting, graduated on time, earned my CPA, and ended up getting an MBA from Northwestern University.

That's four schools in one calendar year if you're scoring at home (five if you include taking history over the summer at Oakton Community College).

When I was going through this, I was riddled with doubt. When I focused on the past, my dad would urge me to look ahead.

"So, you bounced around a bit," he would say. "Who cares? It's what you do now, that's how you'll be measured!"

He tried to lighten the mood. He said I could also be measured with a ruler. It wasn't funny but I appreciated his efforts.

"It's not where you've been; it's where you're going."

Today, I find this phrase helpful with my clients and students. Exactly *every* person I meet has their own unique (financial) backstory. There are some ups and some downs. *Every* single person has a decision he or she would like to undo. We'd all like a mulligan or two.

The trouble surfaces when people are unable (or unwilling) to make positive change toward SECURiMENT because they're stuck in the past. This occurs when the gravitational pull of the status quo keeps you where you are despite the fact that making a few changes would be in your best interest.

For a while at Indiana, I felt that I didn't belong because of my initial struggles and because I no longer had a bicycle, but my dad wasn't having any of that. "Let what you do now define you. Don't look back," he said.

Oh, it's easy to laugh now but we all have a past. Social, financial and otherwise.

Hopefully, the steps you've taken to accumulate your assets

The. Race. Of. Your. Life!

have worked in your favor. But as you near retirement, what you've done in the past has much less importance. It's the choices you make **now** that will define your retirement.

That's just the way it works!

Chapter 9
Get Some Help

After a lifetime of watching football, I now realize that quarterback coaches and financial advisors are very similar. Let me explain! Every quarterback has a minimum of two opponents:

1) Opposing defense that wants to rip his head off, and
2) Himself.

By himself, I'm referring to his "head" and the mistakes that are made in the heat of the game. Throwing off the wrong foot, holding on to the ball too long, or, our favorite here in Chicago, throwing into triple coverage or to players wearing the other team's uniform.

Anyway, a good coach protects his quarterback, not only from tricky defenses, but unforced errors.

Which brings me to the quarterback of your future. YOU!

As the quarterback of your future, you face a ferocious defense (the financial markets) that are very difficult to navigate. As if that wasn't challenging enough, you also have the psychological side of the game.

Many individual investors simply do not have the time, patience, knowledge, or persistence to deal effectively with their investments over the long term. Further, there are common mistakes that they make that a professional advisor can help to overcome:

1) Making ad hoc, fear-based revisions at the first sign of market weakness;

2) Emphasizing individual securities rather than the overall portfolio;

3) Failing to re-evaluate the financial situation at least annually and then revise plans;

4) Getting caught up in market hype and losing investment focus;

5) Chasing investment fads.

Good financial advisors are like coaches. They help their clients understand market risk, diversification, and tax efficiency. But they also save them from making unforced errors.

Sounds about right. But is there a way to quantify the help a good advisor provides?

According to The Vanguard Group, "Advisors can add up to 3 percent per year to client returns by helping them allocate assets, rebalance appropriately, and stick with the program when times are tough which they may be over the next 10 years."

Per *Forbes* magazine:

> *"Lately, I've been encouraging investors to think about and address the possibility of lower portfolio returns over the next few years. But how many people will actually do the research and take action? My guess would be not very many. Most of us are simply too busy with the day-to-day to worry about risks that might not show up for a decade or more. Wow, that's complicated. I'm probably okay. It can wait."*

Even more worrisome, according to *Time* magazine (2015), 81% of investors say expectations for double digit gains going forward are realistic, and 54% believe their portfolios will perform better (going forward) than in a year like 2014, when the Standard & Poor's 500 Index rose by 13% (Natixis Global Asset Management).

Many outlooks suggest lower returns going forward, and we are entering a time where mistakes will cost more than ever before. Managing (minimizing) drawdown will be vital, protecting principal even more so.

The elephant in the room is: Fees. It's true, there are fees. Nobody disputes that advisors earn some money for their efforts.

But what's important to keep in mind is that there are fees in all your investment accounts. Many 401(k)s have high fees. Insurance products have fees, as does nearly every mutual fund. Most people don't realize it because the fees are generally hard to decipher. What you don't see/know, will hurt you.

To me, the real question, which is actually a series of questions, is this: If you're going to pay somebody (which you are), what are you going to get for it? Will they help you devise a plan? Are you going to get sound investment, retirement and tax advice or are you going to get unnecessary and arbitrary fees which are hard to see?

Somebody is going to get paid for something; you might as well get something tangible in return. And at the very least, especially if you are handling your own investments, get a second opinion. Every day, I tell some people that they're doing just fine. They like to hear that. I just wish I could say it more often!

That's just the way it works.

Chapter 10
Keep the Curtains Closed

Has this ever happened to you? After months of work, your long-awaited vacation has arrived. You and your significant other are finally getting some time away. Dinner was wonderful, and the show was mesmerizing. Perhaps the nightcap was unnecessary, but that's a different story.

In the morning, there are no alarms, no responsibilities, no children. As the sun rises, you begin to feel its presence. Slowly at first, but now it's shining through the curtains—the very curtains you remember closing last night. Now, the sun is hitting you right in the eyes. It's nearly impossible to sleep. Although the covers are warm and removing them is the last thing you want to do, somebody must close the curtains.

Unfortunately, they won't close all the way. For some reason, as if it's written in *The Dummies Guide for Hotel Construction* manual, no matter how hard you pull on each side, you just can't seem to get the curtains to close to prevent that growing speck of light from illuminating the room.

Have you been there? (Incidentally, if you google "closing hotel curtains," there are all sorts of interesting remedies.)

Anyway, this is exactly how I view the years leading up to retirement. (Please allow me a little latitude here!)

You may or may not know this, but there is a gap between the period of your life when you're accumulating assets and the time of your life when you're de-accumulating (or spending down) those assets.

It's the time in your life when questions previously ignored and avoided are now front and center. Suddenly, there is a light shining on your future, and, in some cases, it's affecting your sleep.

- How will market volatility affect my retirement?
- Is there a way for me to pay less in taxes? What if I pay too much in taxes?
- Should I be concerned with inflation?
- Will I outlive my money?
- How will my health affect the rest of my life?
- What will happen when I no longer receive a regular paycheck? What happens when there are no more raises? No more bonuses?

It's these questions—these concerns—that interfere with your ability to sleep. To rest. To relax. Figuratively, these burdens are the little specks of light that keep many people up at night.

Keep the curtains closed! (Seamlessly transition between the two stages)

This much is certain. The skills you used to accumulate wealth are different from what you must know to efficiently liquidate wealth. Once, a student in my retirement class told me his advisor said not to worry about de-accumulation—that above-average rates of returns would keep the light out, so to speak. I was shocked because that statement is simply not true.

In retirement, average returns aren't nearly as important as when those returns occur. Negative returns at the beginning of retirement can be devastating. That's just one example. There are many others.

Closing the curtains is about effectively transitioning from accumulation to de-accumulation. It's about transforming from uncertainty to certainty—moving from a vague notion of how to navigate this period of your life to having concrete steps for making solid decisions when they matter the most.

That's just the way it works!

Chapter 11
Know Your Risk Number

Do you know your sleep (risk) number?

If you've shopped for a new mattress, undoubtedly, you've heard or seen the following slogan plastered all over: "What's your Sleep Number®?"

The company behind this question states: *"When you find your ideal Sleep Number® setting, you'll feel aligned, supported and comfortable!"*

You know what else makes for a good night's sleep? Investing in accordance with your risk appetite!

As you know from reading this far, SECURiMENT is about peace of mind. SECURiMENT is about being able to rest—to sleep well both now and in retirement.

It's about feeling aligned, supported, and comfortable. Yes, I realize what I'm suggesting. You should choose your investments the same way you pick out your next mattress.

Seriously, though, everybody has a risk number that corresponds to their comfort level. No two individuals of the same age will have the same asset allocation because the allocation gets defined by their comfort level. This is important for the long term.

So, ascertaining your risk appetite is the first step. Then you have to ask this question: Are you invested according to your risk appetite?

Every portfolio has a risk number! Every stock, every bond, almost anything you can put your money in—each has a risk number. Some people hate market risk and the ups and downs of their investments, while others laugh at it. It's important that you know where you stand — or sleep.

The question is how far a portfolio can fall within a fixed period of time before an investor will capitulate and make an emotionally charged, poor investing decision.

Per Investopedia: *"You should have a realistic understanding of your ability and willingness to stomach large swings in the value of your investments; if you take on too much risk, you might panic and sell at the wrong time."*

Well, that makes sense, and studies bear it out.

As I've mentioned in other parts of this book, numerous studies show that individual investors don't do nearly as well individually as the stock funds they're invested in. Said another way, just because your mutual fund is up 10% doesn't mean you've earned a 10% return for the same period. The DALBAR study is the most commonly cited work on this subject, and you can google and download the report for your education.

It's all about the emotion!

The following passage is from the CFA Institute Research Foundation, a not-for-profit organization established to promote the development and dissemination of relevant research for investment practitioners worldwide:

> "Investment theory assumes a rational investor does make a logical trade-off between the expected return and risk of a portfolio of investments. **But investors are inherently human; hence, emotions will inevitably come into play.** This is particularly true for less sophisticated investors who are not trained in finance and who lack experience with investments. Retail investors and high-net-worth individuals may be emotional about their lifetime savings, yet their advisers often find it difficult to assess how these emotions will be expressed in future financial decisions. This difficulty should come as no surprise, because as human beings we are often surprisingly bad

at identifying emotions."

I like the six-month time frame for measuring risk as a way to reduce the devastation of emotionally charged investing decisions. The six-month time frame is appropriate because most research points to this simple truth: *While investors should be focused on the long term, they react to risk in the short term, and emotional reactions to risk are the number one killer of long-term financial goals and results.*

That's just the way it works!

Chapter 12
Learn Wall Street's Tricks

"Wall Street wants to separate you from your money. What can you do about it?"

Do you understand how Wall Street does things? You'll make better decisions for your retirement plan if you know some of its tricks. This first "practice" below is a biggie!

Arithmetic Returns vs. Chained Returns

This trick focuses on how returns are calculated and reported. You might be surprised to know that there are two methods: Arithmetic returns and chained returns. Arithmetic returns are similar to a simple average; a computation that's probably more familiar to you. But it's chained returns that are most important. Let's look at two scenarios (Table 1 below) from one of my favorite books: *The Capitalist's Lament - How Wall Street Is Fleecing You and Ruining America*.

	Column One	Column Two	Column Three	Column Four
	Annual Rate of Return	Arithmetic Return	Chained Return	Value of $100 Investment After Each Year
Year 1	48%	48%	48%	$148.00
Year 2	<35%>	6.5%	<1.9%>	$96.20
Year 3	15%	9.3%	3.5%	$110.63
Year 4	<12%>	4%	<0.65%>	$97.35

Table 1. Progression of Value: Arithmetic Return vs. Chained Return.

The arithmetic return (Column 2) suggests that your average return is 4% per year, which is calculated by adding the previous years' numbers and dividing by four (Add up the percentages in Column 1 and divide by 4.) With a 4% average increase per year, you might think your balance increased 16% (4% times 4 years), which would be higher than when you started, but that's not the case. Due to massive performance swings, you surprisingly have $2.65 less than when you started. (You started with $100 and ended with $97.35!)

With a simple average, you're not doing too poorly. With the chained (or actual) result – not so good. (The calculation is as follows: Take $100 and increase by 48%, decrease by 35%, increase by 15%, then decrease by 12%. You'll be left with $97.35!) That's not so good!

Whatever Wall Street wants to pretend, you live in the *chained* world. (You lost $2.65 and, more importantly, 4 years.) This is another reason why a *tortoise* approach to accumulating assets is preferable to a *hare* approach. The tortoise wins again! If the gains and losses from years 1 and 2 were smaller, the result would have been much better.

Much of the Good Performance Has Already Happened

This sleight of hand trick focuses on how big mutual fund companies choose which funds make it to prime time and are offered to investors. For every fund offered to investors, many more are kept on the shelf. This process is known as, "incubation." It's misleading because investors are led to believe that all of a company's offerings are top-notch. They don't show you the ones that perform poorly. As if that weren't bad enough, often, a fund's great performance occurs before mainstream investors get involved. A fund has some early success, but then reverts to the mean and returns become ordinary – or worse. Thankfully, for the company (but not you), by then there are enough investors generating ample profits. Just because a fund has a positive track record doesn't mean YOU will benefit after investing YOUR money.

Positivity Sells, Pessimism Doesn't

In 2000, *Fortune* magazine ran an article titled, "The Top Picks From Wall Street." The gist of its findings was that Wall Street analysts issue many more buy recommendations than sell recommendations. "Analysts made 33,169 stock recommendations the prior year. Of those, only 125 were recommendations that you sell that stock or approximately .34 percent (1 in 300)." *Fortune* isn't alone here. Many publications and studies offer the same result for a multitude of reasons. For example, if Fidelity Investments places a buy rating on your favorite company, it may not be because it thinks it will go up in price. It could be for another reason. Most investors don't know that many of the financial firms that issue *buy* ratings also do other business with the companies being rated. Think about it. If you're an investment bank, It's not wise to issue a sell rating (thus causing a stock price to fall) in one breath and ask for advisory or banking business with the next! (Follow the money!)

Once again – from *The Capitalist's Lament:*

> *"Despite how things turn out, there is a tremendous bias towards optimism. Wall Street insiders will not offer advice that will adversely affect their own incomes, and their customers don't want to hear bad news. Who's going to buy stocks and other securities after being told that values will decline?"*

Some Latin may help here. *Caveat Emptor* – let the buyer beware.

That's just the way it works!

Chapter 13
Leave Predictions to the Weather Forecaster

Every family has inside jokes. We have a new one. You may find it silly, but for us, one innocuous line has provided a few laughs. It started on our holiday vacation when I asked Josh (my oldest) what he wanted to do that day.

"I don't know, dad. I'm not a future-teller." My two younger sons, Danny and Ben, joined in when I suggested we get coffee in a few minutes. "We're not future-tellers, dad..." (Does that mean you don't want coffee? How about a little help here!)

I didn't realize you needed a crystal ball to answer such a perplexing question. So, let it be noted, there are two entities that don't predict the future very well. My family and, apparently, most economic and market forecasters.

John Mauldin, well-known economist, stated:
> *"One might think that all our newfangled technology would make forecasting the future a little easier. I read just last week that scientists have devised electrical wires only three atoms thick. Imagine how powerful a computer chip made with that wiring will be. Yet all our computing horsepower still can't predict worth a darn what Washington or Wall Street will do to us this year. In fact, there is convincing evidence is that every model that forecasters use is really bad at forecasting, beyond giving us a vague sense of direction."*

Indeed, the models aren't very good. This much we know. But there is something else to know. It's a business (the financial engine), and most of the information (marketing) we ingest is designed to fit us with rose-colored glasses.

Lance Roberts, an economist at www.realinvestmentadvice.com:
> *"We can't predict the future – if it was actually possible fortune tellers would all win the lottery. They don't, we*

can't, and we aren't going to try. However, this doesn't stop the annual parade of Wall Street analysts from pegging 12-month price targets on the S&P 500 as if there was an actual science behind what is nothing more than a 'WAG' (Wild Ass Guess)."

At the end of 2016, Barron's investment strategists from all the big houses (Goldman Sachs, Black Rock, etc.) issued all their predictions for 2017. Not one of these experts saw the market falling — even by just a little bit. This on the heels of an eight-year-period where the market indexes increased substantially and stock prices were considered "very expensive." I was flabbergasted. Maybe these strategists didn't want to go out on a limb and be the only one predicting even the slightest decrease!

Pessimism doesn't help these companies that benefit when investors stay invested and excited about the markets. The result is that investors stay interested, aggressive, and even optimistic when they should be 1) Reducing exposure to stocks if conditions warrant, or 2) Proactively managing their potential downside, 3) Or both!

Here is a quote from *The Capitalists Lament - How Wall Street Is Fleecing You and Ruining America* that gets to the heart of what's wrong with making predictions about the market:

> "For Wall Street experts, optimism is simply more profitable. As a prognosticator, if you're right, you're heaped with adulation. Being wrong (but optimistic) begets acceptance. Unfortunately, it's far worse on the other side. Being realistic and wrong gets you fired."

Which leads me to an overarching point: Take all predictions with a grain of salt. Be wary when others aren't, and be aggressive when others are afraid. Manage your downside risk. The bane of your investing existence isn't missing out on great years in the stock market. It's suffering, then slowly recovering from the terrible years.

That's just the way it works!

Chapter 14
Manage the Max Drawdown

I recently read an article titled, "Level-headed strategies for volatile markets." One of the points regarding investing was "Don't be tempted by emotion." I thought that was a little glib because for anybody planning to retire within the next several years, emotion will always be a factor.

As I type this, there is a lot of uncertainty in the world. The news is on in the background, and it's speaking about Covid and all kinds of mayhem in the world. The stock market is on an eight-year bull run, which has the market, by many measures, as overvalued as it was before the crashes of 1929 and 2008. I could go on and on.

Volatility makes for stressful investing. Unfortunately, trying to time when to exit or enter markets is very difficult and not likely to work out in your favor. Research shows that investors are notoriously terrible at predicting market tops and bottoms. Corrections happen regularly, and periods of high growth often occur close to major pullbacks. If you're not in the market when it rallies, you may miss out on the best days of performance.

Here's how I remove emotion from the equation. I minimize the max. That is, I *manage the max drawdown*. Let me explain. When evaluating performance, many investors look at percentage weighted returns - achieving 10% in the stock market or beating the S&P 500 or Barkley's Bond Index by a few percentage points. Instead, look at the dollar returns because, in the end, it's dollars that pay for cars, homes, food, etc.

One way to *maximize dollar returns* is to minimize the amount your portfolio drops when markets take a turn for the worst.

Here's an example. I recently stress tested my father's portfolio to see how his investments would fare if markets were to drop as they did in 2008. I wanted to see how his investments would perform in a worst-case scenario. The reason this is important to my dad is because he is 84 years old and lives off his investments. If the markets, and subsequently his investments, drop off a financial cliff, he'll be liquidating assets for normal spending needs at depressed levels. That's how portfolios get decimated and retirements get ruined.

My dad's current portfolio computed a max drawdown a bit above 26%. To provide some perspective, in the last market meltdown (2008), the S & P 500 dropped approximately 53% from its highest point to its lowest point. So, a reading of 26% for dad's portfolio didn't strike me as terrible considering how the markets have performed at their worst. But it got me thinking - what if we could achieve the same expected return, but with a max drawdown of less than 11%. Now, we're taking much less risk for the same return, which will naturally remove some emotion from the equation.

I don't remember where I read the following quote, but it pretty much sums up my thinking here:

> "Big money knows that investing is more about balancing risk and reward than about being 'right!' Investing is a game of probability and since nobody has a crystal ball, the best we can do is make educated guesses that minimize our risk."

So ask your financial advisor about your max drawdown and challenge this individual to minimize your downside risk – without reducing your returns. When things get dicey, stop listening to the noise. Turn off the television, throw away the business section, and stay off financial Web sites. That will only add to your stress and encourage emotional decision making. Instead, develop a strategy for marginalizing downside risk, and you'll sleep better.

That's just the way it works!

Chapter 15
Protect Your Principal

The average American faces a real dilemma when heading into retirement. We have limited time to invest until we retire, and the financial marketing machine is feeding us information that is not helpful. We've been bombarded with advice advocating "long-term investing," but nobody accurately defines "long term."

It's really "TIME" that we should focus on, as in - *how long do YOU have until retirement?*

If it's less than 15-20 years, you may have a serious problem. There are numerous periods in history where returns over a 20-year period have been very poor. For example, people who retired in 1999 experienced incredible returns in the late 90's. They went out on top! On the other hand, those who retired in 2008 during the Great Recession, experienced something different all together.

Enough of the past, let's get back to the present. We haven't had recession yet this decade. But, at some point, it's going to happen. Without further injections from the Federal Reserve to boost asset prices, stocks will go lower. During an average recessionary period, stocks lose, on average, 33% of their value.

Such a decline would set most investors back more than five years from their investment goals...which brings up another question.

> *Do you have enough time before retirement to take such a hit and still achieve your retirement goals?*

Please allow me another running analogy. I saw this investing quote in the *Chicago Tribune*.

> *The long run is your long run!*

Here's my take on the whole *long run* terminology. It's easy to project decent stock market returns over a long time period, but what does that really mean for YOU? Your *"long run"* is likely much shorter than the time horizon over which most investing stats are computed. Your *long run* may be more like a short 5K (3.1 miles) road race, rather than a full marathon.

As an investor, you must have a well-thought-out investment plan to deal with periods of heightened financial market turmoil. Decisions to move in and out of an asset class must be made logically and unemotionally. Benjamin Graham, legendary author of *The Intelligent Investor* said, "The investor's chief problem – and even his worst enemy – is likely to be himself." Don't let that be you.

Don't sabotage your own retirement! For long-term success, have a disciplined portfolio review process that considers how various assets should be allocated to suit your investment objectives, risk tolerance, and time frame.

Massive losses or drawdowns AND emotional decisions must be avoided at all costs.

Emotions and investment decisions don't play together nicely. Retail investors, especially during a bull (or rising) market, often use generic asset-allocation models that are heavily weighted in equities under the illusion that, over a long enough period, they will somehow make enough money.

Unfortunately, history has been a brutal teacher on the value of risk management and what goes down may take a long time to come back. The following points show how much of an increase is needed to recover from steep declines:

1) 20% drop in the market requires a 25% increase to get back to even;

2) 30% drop in the market requires a 42% increase to get back to even;

3) 50% drop in the market requires a 100% increase to get back to even.

I don't want to ruin your day, but we've had two 50% drops this century. First in 2000 with the dot.com bust and then with the great recession of 2007-2009. You know what they say about people who ignore history…they're doomed to repeat it, or just doomed…

Even small drawdowns require a great percentage gain to break even. Hopefully, the message is clear. PROTECT YOUR PRINCIPAL!
It's not what you have now, it's what will be available when you retire. Stock prices spend an inordinate amount of time getting back to even. In 2000, the S&P hit 2,048 and didn't reach that milestone again until 2014. That's 14 years spent trying to make up lost ground. Trying to get back to even. The Vanguard S&P 500 index fund (VFINX) has $531 billion of your dollars. If the markets go sideways or up and down over the next several years, there will be lot of people stuck in quicksand, desperately trying to claw their way back to even, and . . .

Getting back to even is not a successful strategy. **It is always easier to regain a lost opportunity. It is far more difficult to regain lost capital!**

That's just the way it works!

Chapter 16
Raise Some Cash

I've passed the 50-yard line in life, and I feel that the next big market run will be key for my retirement. The current bull market where stock prices have been rising has raged on for what seems like forever. More than ten years to be exact, but it will end at some point.

It always does.

Sometime, down the road, there will be an extremely attractive time to buy the stocks of great companies, sectors, or indexes at prices that are much more appealing than today. The key is: When? Nobody knows. That's why the financial industry is full of professionals exhorting you to stay invested all the time.

Let's examine why this is the case.

Simply, financial service firms make more money when you're fully invested. They spread language like the following, which is from a *Wall Street Journal* (*WSJ*) piece titled, "The Market Timing Myth."

> *"For years, the investment industry has tried to scare clients into staying fully invested in the stock market at all times, no matter how high stocks go or what's going on in the economy. 'You can't time the market,' they warn. 'Studies show that market timing doesn't work'."*

And they trot out a well-known fact of how terrible your returns would be if you missed out on the biggest (best) stock market days. This is correct. Returns are negatively affected when you sit out the big days.

However, we know due to research and human behavior that stock market investors are an emotional breed. Many of us buy when we should sell and sell when we should buy. Those psychological forces are often to blame. The result is that when markets rise in euphoric times as they have since the 2016 election, investors continue to plow money into investments they manage passively with no help from professionals. Then, when markets fall and they grow weary of tears soaking their brokerage statements, they sell at the wrong time.

You clearly don't want to miss the big days, but that's only half the story. What about the disastrous days? Would it help to sit out the bloodiest days? A finance professor from a school in Spain studied this dilemma. Per the *WSJ* article:

> "Over an investing period of about 40 years, he calculated, missing the 10 best days would have cost you about half your capital gains. But successfully avoiding the 10 worst days would have had an even bigger positive impact on your portfolio. Someone who avoided the 10 biggest slumps would have ended up with two and a half times the capital gains of someone who simply stayed in all the time."

Missing the bad days will help your returns!

Market timing doesn't work, so give that strategy a pass. I always have at least 30% of my portfolio in equities at all times because markets move faster than I do. To me, having 100% cash or equities is a mistake.

Use positive (upward) price action to raise cash. In other words, sell the rallies; the times when the market goes higher and you can take some profits. At the very least, use times of incredible strength to rebalance your portfolio. Although it may not seem intuitive, if you aim for a certain split (i.e. 60% stocks/40% bonds), use these opportunities to rebalance to your ideal allocation. Currently, I'm seeing a lot of retirement accounts that are out of balance because stocks have increased so much in the last three or four months. Rebalancing forces you to sell some of the winners, which will help you in the long run.

That's just the way it works!

Chapter 17
Reduce Investment Volatility

Recently, I flew to Charlotte with my son Ben. The flight was bumpy. Very bumpy. So turbulent that the flight attendants took their seats before giving the lady across the aisle her Tito's, with a slice of lime—at 9 a.m.

It's always five o'clock somewhere, right?

Anyway, I used to like the bumps—or at least not mind them as much. During the flight, Ben hunkered down with whatever he was doing on his computer, but I closed my eyes, practiced my deep breathing, and yearned for calmer skies.

At this point in my life, there are two activities in which I do not enjoy volatility: air travel and investments.

What I know about SECURiMENT is that there comes a time when market volatility is no longer your friend. When you were younger, it was more acceptable. You had time to kill! Retirement was down yonder a few years.

But as you near or enjoy retirement, you have reached a point in time when it is no longer acceptable to lose money and when maximum drawdown should be greatly reduced. Maximum drawdown is the vertical distance from the value of your portfolio at its highest point to the amount left over at its lowest.

There comes a time when it makes sense to build a foundation or construct a floor under a portion of your assets. Simply, there comes a time when the value of some of your assets should not go any lower. Period. End of sentence.

See, it's easy when things are going well!

Do you know the expression, "A rising tide lifts all boats"? All funds look good in an up market. Many advisors look good in an up market. It's easy to buy and hold in an up market, but there comes a point when taking the least amount of risk to achieve your desired rate of return is advised—whatever rate helps you achieve SECURiMENT.

When markets fluctuate wildly, individual investors generally earn too little reward per unit of risk. You may remember this. Between 2005 and 2012, the average rate of return of the S&P was 4.9%, but the drawdown risk was 55%. From top to bottom, the S&P fell 55%. That's too much risk, because when markets drop sharply, the average investor is incapable of the *holding* part of buy-and-hold investing. Sadly, short-term mistakes ruin long-term retirement plans.

If you don't believe me, google "Dalbar."

DALBAR, Inc., is the nation's leading financial services market research firm and performs a variety of ratings and evaluations of practices within the financial services industry. Every year, they determine that the average stock investor doesn't do nearly as well as the average stock fund he or she invests in.

For example, in 2016, the average equity mutual fund investor underperformed the S&P 500 by a margin of -4.70%. While the broader market made gains of 11.96%, the average equity investor earned only 7.26% (DALBAR, *Quantitative Analysis of Investor Behavior 2016*). Their analysis from 2017 to 2020 is similar.

What causes this underperformance? In a word: emotion. What causes emotion? Volatility.

What I know about achieving SECURiMENT is that there comes a point in time when volatility, drawdowns, and market losses aren't much fun anymore! The younger set might appreciate the bumps, but you and I -not so much!

That's just the way it works.

Chapter 18
Run Your Own Race

A few years back, I had a goal of playing the keyboard. I love listening to music. I love singing, too. Although my voice has never been described as smooth and velvety (My last glass of cabernet, maybe. But not my voice.)

In hopes of being more musical, I purchased a keyboard. I started with a catchy, yet challenging, classic: "Mary Had a Little Lamb." My son, Danny, who was 16 years old at the time, also tried playing. He chose a far more intricate song. While I was hunting and pecking at the keys in what seemed like slow motion, Danny was quickly kicking it into high gear. Before long, he had the first several verses of his (more difficult) song under control. I was still looking for "B flat."

Watching him get up to speed so much more quickly than me, I felt disappointed (maybe even a bit disillusioned). My inner voice was having a field day! But, over time, I've learned that whether it's running, playing the keyboard, or watching stock market indexes, comparisons can get you into trouble.

Once again, from www.RealInvestmentAdvice.com:

> *"Comparison in the financial arena is the main reason investors have trouble patiently sitting on their hands, letting whatever process they are comfortable with work for them. They get waylaid by some comparison along the way and lose their focus. If you tell investors that they made 12% on their account, they are very pleased. If you subsequently inform them that 'everyone else' made 14%, you have made them upset!"*

In other words, run your own race! Develop a retirement plan with a reasonable rate of return that considers not only your risk tolerance, but how the market is priced. There is no rule that says you must be 100% invested in equities - 100% of the time. Your goal, always, is to manage the maximum drawdown or how far down your money goes when the tide turns and the market takes a hit. It's not the up years that should concern you, it's the down years. You likely won't beat the market averages, and there are several reasons why:

1) Indexes don't have cash - but you do. (Most investors carry some cash, which reduces returns.)

2) Indexes don't have a life expectancy - but you do. (The index operates on its own time table. You have only so many years until retirement.)

3) Indexes don't compensate for distributions to meet living requirements - but you do. Indexes don't figure in if you have home improvements to do or if you take your grandchildren on vacation.

4) Indexes have no associated taxes, costs, or other expenses - but you have all of those.

5) Indexes can substitute at no penalty - but you don't get penalty free changes to your portfolio. This is the biggest difference of them all. For example, when the market cap of an S&P 500 company falls, it is just miraculously replaced in the index. If you own the same company and it declines, you suffer the consequences. You don't get a mulligan as it were - to coin a golf phrase. A do over. Just try that trick with your stockbroker when things go south.

You Can't Compare Indexes

Index averages are a different animal. Another factor is which index you are looking at. The Dow Jones Industrial Average contains just 30 stocks. The S&P 500 has, you guessed it, the stocks of 500 companies. If your portfolio is well-diversified, it may have 10,000 different companies. Big, small, in America, overseas. There is simply no way to compare. The bottom line is that chasing returns or comparing indexes are behaviors that cause investors to take on more risk. A better strategy is to "run your own race" by determining a reasonable rate of return for your retirement goals and sticking to a strategy that gets you there in one piece.

That's just the way it works!

Chapter 19
Save More

Riddle me this, Batman! What do YOU (a private investor) and the largest pension plan in the United States have in common? I promise this is not a trick question!

There are two ways for investors and pension plans to reach their retirement goals. CalPERS (California Public Employees' Retirement System) is the largest pension plan in the country. It is an agency in the California executive branch that manages pension and health benefits for more than 1.6 million public employees, retirees, and their families in the state.

It promises school teachers, firefighters, police officers, and other state employees that: If they work a certain number of years, they will receive a monthly pension check for the rest of their lives. Sounds like a great deal, right? Well, a proposed change by CalPERS may mean major consequences. In December 2016, the *Wall Street Journal* reported the following:

> "California Public Employees' Retirement System plans to propose that its board abandon a long-held goal of achieving a 7.5% (annual rate of return) and reduce it to 7.25% or 7%, to start aligning its rate of return expectations with reality.

> "A reduction in CalPERS' return target to 7% or 7.25% would have real-life consequences for taxpayers and cities. It would likely trigger a painful increase in yearly pension bills for the towns, counties, and school districts that participate in California's state pension plan. Any loss in expected investment earnings must be made up with significantly higher annual contributions from public employers as well as the state.

> "If the assumed rate of return fell to 7%, the state and school districts participating in CalPERS would have to pay

at least $15 billion more over the next 20 years," said Amy Morgan, spokesperson. "That number doesn't include cities and local agencies."

Though none of you are probably affected by what happens with CalPERS, this is not good for any of us. CalPERS has the best and brightest minds managing its money. Even with all that firepower, it is still being forced to reduce expected future returns.

What does this mean? The ripple effect through California would be brutal with ramifications from the Redwoods to San Diego. Municipalities would be forced to kick more into the plan because they can't earn enough return on their invested assets. For example, consider the amount necessary to pay benefits in 10 years. If you assume a higher rate of return, you can tolerate having less money today because the investment gains will bridge the gap. With smaller growth rates and the same amount required in 10 years – you must have MORE now because it won't grow as much.

As a private investor, what does this mean for you? It goes back to the answer to the riddle: There are two ways for investors and pension plans to reach their retirement goals.
    1) Earn a higher investment rate of return, or
    2) Save more money each year

I bet you can see where this is going!

Option #1, monkeying around with rates of return, is easier to fathom because saving more is simply not palatable to mere mortals or municipalities. However, squeezing a few extra points of investment return each year is much easier to digest.

Noted economist, Lance Roberts, puts it succinctly:

> "You cannot INVEST your way to your retirement goal. As this century should have taught you by now, the stock market is not a 'get wealthy for retirement' scheme. You cannot continue to under save for your retirement hoping the

> *stock market will make up the difference. As stated, this is the same trap that pension funds across this country have fallen into and are now paying the price for."*

So, that's what you (as an investor) and many pension funds have in common. Neither is probably saving enough. Both need to sock more away on a yearly basis. Nobody, and I mean nobody, wants Option #3 - having less money in the end.

That's just the way it works!

Chapter 20
Set Realistic Targets

Back when I was running marathons, I would often use an online pace calculator to help me predict my time in the next big race. This calculator would take times from a shorter distance, like a 5K race or half-marathon, and predict my marathon time. Quickly, I learned that the farther I had run at verifiable pace in a race (i.e. a half-marathon), the more likely the calculator would spit out something reasonable and attainable for longer distances. With the shorter distances (3.1 miles), it felt more arbitrary. (Think junk in...junk out.)

Pacing calculators remind me of what it's like to use a retirement calculator. You may be familiar with how these tools work as they're all over the Internet. Typical inputs are rate of investment return, rate of inflation, years until retirement, and expenses (spending) in retirement. Just a few keystrokes and presto, you'll know how long your money will last! Sadly, most of these variables are relative unknowns with varying levels of, well, variability. Most people can take a reasonable stab at years until retirement, spending and rate of inflation, but it's the estimate that investors use for rate of return that scares me. That's why it can be helpful to look at historical trends (See Table 2 below).

30-Year Period	Annualized Return Before Inflation	Annualized Return After Inflation
1960-1989	10.30%	5.07%
1970-1999	13.78%	8.24%
1980-2009	11.29%	7.52%

Table 2. *Historical Trends in Annualized Returns*
(Source: www.moneyunder30.com)

The. Race. Of. Your. Life!

Somebody might look at the chart above and think 10% seems reasonable, but I do have two concerns right off the bat with using returns this high. (I categorize any return greater than 6% as too high for your retirement calculator!)

These figures assume that you invested your money at the exact beginning of these periods and let the money sit unfettered until the exact end of the period. This is highly unlikely. Rarely does money sit this long (untouched), and the rate of return you experience has much more to do with the exact time the bulk of your savings is invested.

That gives me pause, but the next point keeps me up at night.

These are dramatically different times! After all, we have experienced two cataclysmic bear markets in this century. As you know, during a bear market, prices fall and widespread pessimism causes the stock market's downward spiral to be self-sustaining. During these periods, it's not a particularly pleasant time to be an investor and, yes, there have been two brutal BEAR markets in recent memory.

So, if you ignore modern history, you will be doing it at your own retirement peril. For a more relevant period (2000 – 2016), the actual compound rate of return is a more pedestrian 4.47%, which includes dividends being reinvested.

Let me explain. This assumes that you have been invested in a fund that follows the S&P 500 to a tee and you choose to let all the dividends reinvest. Further, we assume that you were invested in this index for the entire period. What if you only owned 20 stocks and they didn't pay dividends as often or as much. Would your return be affected? Absolutely. If we change our inputs a bit and assume no dividends, the return drops to 2.51%. Even if we meet in the middle and choose 3.5%, you'll see it has not been a very good century for stocks. It's not the retirement calculator, it's the inputs. Garbage in, garbage out.

What rate of return do I use in my calculations? I use 5 to 6% for the following two reasons.

First, it's more in line with what's happening in this century and doesn't harken back to a time before my children were born. Second, and more importantly, if the numbers don't look as rosy (because of more realistic assumptions), my clients will save more. And that will be better for the long run – no matter what the retirement calculator tells you.

That's just the way it works!

Chapter 21
Simplify Your Plan

I know you've heard the following expression:

> *Money can't buy you happiness, but smart financial decisions will buy you SECURiMENT!*

Well, you've heard it now!

All lame jokes aside once people learn the SECURiMENT Method, their first thoughts are usually along these lines: "Where do I begin?" or "What should be tackled first?" or "How should I proceed?"

It can be overwhelming, and, because people are living longer, more risks are coming into play.

- The risk that you won't have enough income
- The risk that market volatility will damage your plans
- The risk that a major health event will sap your savings
- The risk that inflation will reduce your purchasing power
- The risk that you'll pay too much income tax
- The risk that you'll either spend too much or too little

That last bullet point might carry the most weight, as it pertains to your happiness. Really, I don't know which is worse: spending too much of your nest egg too soon and running out of money later in life or spending too little and experiencing the opposite. Spending too little in retirement.

I call that imprisonment. It's being on the outside looking in on what might have been—the trips you might have taken, the hobbies you might have pursued, the causes you might have supported if you'd felt you had the resources.

Here's how I view this: secure income = SECURiMENT.

The. Race. Of. Your. Life!

One day in the future, you're going to get tired of working—if it hasn't happened already. Unfortunately, your bills will *not* get tired of being paid!

So, at the root of your entire financial future is income, which is why it occupies such a large part of the SECURiMENT Method.

Multiple sources of steady income will allow you to pay your bills. Plain and simple.

There's your rent. Food and medicine. Clothing. You know, the necessities. Sure, we all want funds for the discretionary part of retirement, like leisure activities, travel, and helping your children and grandchildren (if you like them). All that stuff. But at the core, you must be in a position to pay your bills.

Simplify your plan.

Your first step is to determine how wide the gap is between your income from guaranteed sources and your expenses.

The second step is determining how that gap might change over time. As you know, your lifestyle choices and health care needs will change during your retirement years. In addition, some discretionary expenses may decline over time in retirement. The only constant is that there will be changes as you navigate your way through the years.

Simplify. Create income.

I find the following to be the best sources of regular income:

1) Social Security
2) Pensions (if you are so fortunate!)
3) Income annuities
4) Dividend stocks

Each has pros and cons, but my aim is not to discuss that here. The aim is to help you focus on what's most important.

To the extent you employ any of the means above, you will be bridging the gap between income and expenses.

The smaller the gap, the less likely it is that you will be forced to make complex financial decisions as you age. And that's a good thing.

Focus on the income, because without it, nothing else matters.

As former *Wall Street Journal* columnist Jonathan Clements famously said:

> "Retirement is like a long vacation in Las Vegas. The goal is to enjoy it to the fullest, but not so fully that you run out of money."

I wish it were so simple. It can be!

That's just the way it works!

Chapter 22
Slay The Silent Retirement Killer

I often ask people if they want to retire with *cash in the bank* and *fuel in the tank*! That's my goal for you. So, if you'll indulge me, I'd like to explain exactly what that means and what can get in the way. Obviously, having cash in the bank will help your retirement, but what about fuel in the tank?

When you finish a race with fuel in the tank, the aftermath is far sweeter and much less painful. Believe me that the post-race party is much better if you have the physical and mental wherewithal to enjoy it! Unfortunately, there are many risks that have the potential to ruin your retirement party. Here is a partial list:

1) Inflation Risk: You will lose purchasing power because of inflation.

2) Market Risk: Your investments will lose value with market swings.

3) Long-term Care Risk: A long-term health event will eat up your savings.

4) Sequence of Returns Risk: The markets won't cooperate as you near retirement; causing you to spend too much of your nest egg in the early years.

5) Tax Rate Risk: Taxes will be significantly higher in the future.

I know what you're thinking, this list is great fun! Not! Unfortunately, there are more where these came from. Those risks have the potential to zap your fuel as you reach the Finish Line of your working years. And, as insidious as they are, they don't compare to the most subtle risk of them all - the risk of inertia or doing nothing.

The. Race. Of. Your. Life!

In the introduction to *The. Race. Of. Your. Life!*, I mentioned the importance of having a retirement plan. But I tried to make it perfectly clear that a 300-page manuscript wasn't necessary. Just a roadmap to get you where you want to go, from where you are now.

Clearly, when it comes to investing for retirement, valuable advice is: DON'T focus on the day-to-day market blips. Unfortunately, U.S. savers (per *U.S. News & World Report*) have taken that suggestion a bit too far.

> *"Instead of avoiding daily monitoring of plans, many Americans are ignoring their savings – or don't even have a strategy. According to a recent survey from Voya Financial, 80 percent of those with retirement plans have avoided reviewing or making any changes over the past year. "That's compared to 43 percent of the respondents making changes to a phone, cable, or Internet plan."*

In full disclosure, I did change my cable package a few years back. Strangely, it was my 24-year-old son, Josh, who was most startled that Sponge Bob was no longer available. He's an airplane pilot who didn't even live with us – so figure that one out!

Anyway, I'm not going to spout all sorts of stats as to how little most Americans have saved for retirement. If you've read this far, you may be in better shape than most. I do want to leave you with the immortal words of Sir Issac Newton's first law of motion – sometimes referred to as the Law of Inertia.

> *An object at rest stays at rest, and an object in motion stays in motion with the same speed and in the same direction unless acted upon by an unbalanced force.*

If your existing plans are at rest and insufficient for the long haul, please do something. The REAL silent retirement killer isn't what's in the plan, it's NOT having a plan.

That's just the way it works!

Chapter 23
Stay on Course

I didn't enter this race for the thrill of victory. I simply wanted to run a local race with some friends. So, one Sunday morning, I toed the line at the ultra-prestigious Deerfield Dash 10K and 5K. It was a recreational crowd. Lots of people running with their children and dogs, a guy wearing a velvet sweatsuit in the middle of summer, and some runners carrying steaming cups of latte.

There weren't too many serious runners. (By the way, I didn't see anybody smoking a cigarette on the start line. I've seen that before which, I have to say, caught me off guard!)

Anyway, the race started and, after a few hundred yards, I realized that I was in first place - a position completely new to me. I came in second place once – and yes, there were more than two runners. There I was, right behind the police car. Could this be the day? Could I be destined for Deerfield Dash greatness? Was I going to be forever immortalized in the Winner's Circle – making me someone the locals would talk about for years to come? Would I be on the cover of the *Deerfield Review*? Would my finisher's photo be tweeted and retweeted? Would I have something to post on my Facebook page besides what I ate for breakfast? (The "likes" would be off the charts!)

Ok, ok. I'll get on with the story.

The police car continued with the 10K route, while I followed the 5K route—all by myself. There were no other runners in sight, and, you guessed it—that's when the trouble started.

I reached the proverbial fork in the road: A four-way intersection with no signs. And yes, I went the wrong way. Instead of going straight, I turned. I don't think even the scarecrow from *The Wizard of Oz* could have saved me that day.

The. Race. Of. Your. Life!

Needless to say, a map would have helped me know where to go. (At least I got a free T-shirt...)

So do you have a course map (a plan) for the busy race known as your financial future? Or, are you running ragged without a clue of how to get to your retirement goals? If you have a plan, *review it regularly*. We don't live in a static world. Things change. One year, you may need to put a new roof on the house. The next year, the market might suffer a mighty correction, which may affect how you meet your spending needs. The point is that a course map will be loaded with course corrections.

Every year, spend time accessing what has transpired, what it means, and what needs to be changed in your plan so you *don't take a wrong turn*. Each year, decisions should be made in an effort to extend the longevity of your assets based on what's happening in the markets or in your personal life.

I hope you experience the opposite than my day at the "Deerfield Dash." I went from euphoria to embarrassment in the blink of a wrong turn. After a few minutes, I realized something was a tad amiss. My watch suggested I had run more than 3.1 miles, which is not a good thing if you haven't finished a race that equals 3.1 miles and you can't see the finish line! I was finally able to re-join the correct course in time to come in 3rd place.

Yes, I know this begs the question. You went off course but still came in third place? The competition was terrible. I didn't say it was the World Championships! The guy who came in 2nd place was a man pushing a twin baby jogger! Ouch! You'd think the diaper bag would have slowed him down ...

Anyway, I wish I had looked at the course map because glory might have been mine. And it can be yours as well during your retirement years, as long as you stay on course!

That's just the way it works!

Chapter 24
Stay Out of the Whackosphere!

Recently, I stumbled on a YouTube channel produced by a self-proclaimed (financial) Social Justice Warrior—whatever that means. The creator described his channel as consumer protection for the masses. (Thank you, I think...)

There were opinion videos on all manner of subject. Annuities, life Insurance, gold, The "4%" rule, real estate investments, stocks, bonds, commodities...

Plus views on actively-managed funds, passively-managed funds, index funds, funds of funds, promissory notes, and more...

The "warrior" also sees himself quite the commentator on current and historical events.

There were numerous videos on Donald Trump, the 2016 election, climate change, the military, health care, Hillary, Congress, the EPA, World War I and II and Trump (again).

He debunked myths, fantasies, legends, fables, superstitions...

He had a thought on so many subjects. I was mesmerized; even a little impressed at first. How could one person possibly have an informed opinion on so many subjects?

Then it occurred to me: it's not possible, certainly when it comes to retirement planning tools.

Reputable professionals study, review and analyze retirement solutions day and night. The changes come fast and furious. Solutions evolve, opportunities develop, and markets do what markets do.

Keeping up to speed is a challenge.

The. Race. Of. Your. Life!

Back to the justice warrior. I wasn't able to ascertain his qualifications. Was he a CPA? A RICP? (Retirement Income Certified Professional) I know he mocked Certified Financial Professionals (CFP's) in one of his videos. Don't you have to take like 7 tests for that accreditation?

My guess is that he's not a financial professional. He's just someone doing the people's work and out to hold companies and industries accountable.

I wonder if he wears a suit at his computer, or just a superhero cape? (Or just his underwear…)

Yes, I'm being tongue and cheek right now. Even a bit chippy. It's because I find it incredulous that people with no business giving guidance, dupe so many into relying on them.

It's serious. There are people who watch this drivel; individuals who absorb this nonsense. Future retirees who rely on bombastic, hysterical (mostly uninformed) opinions.

See, our superhero doesn't need to be certified. He doesn't have a fiduciary duty to anyone, nor does he need to pass an exam(s) to keep his licenses up to date. Yearly training requirements? I don't think so.

What he says out loud isn't regulated or monitored. What I reviewed in these videos and others like them is factually wrong on so many levels. Further, the videos are out there on the web forever.

Stay Out of the Whackosphere!

Forever!

Someone who watches a video 3, 5, 7 years later, doesn't know that solutions have evolved. What may have been a drawback, previously, may be a reason to consider something now.

This guy doesn't have to step out from behind his keyboard, put his pants on and help people plan (and do what is necessary financially) to help them achieve peace-of-mind in retirement.

Here's my turn as warrior in charge of consumer protection. Find and listen to an advisor you like or trust. Or listen to me instead. Yes, I'm compensated for what I do. I tried working for free, but my wife didn't approve. Neither did the boys. They like food. Lots of food!.

Or don't listen to me. That's fine; maybe our philosophies are not aligned. That's cool. Allow me this running analogy. (Here we go with another running reference!)

Everyone one I meet, everyone I teach, you're all runners trying to make it to the finish line. The line that separates work from play. Your first career from your next career. Retirement. Run the race correctly and you get peace of mind in the end. Maybe even a banana.

Me, I'm like the race director. There are lots of runners; lots of races in my world but you only have one. You only have one race.

This IS the race of your life!

So, for entertainment maybe, or to see how the other half lives spend as much time as you want in the far reaches of the Internet. However, when it comes to a subject as important as your retirement, stay away from the Whackosphere! You'll be happy you did.

That's just the way it works!

Chapter 25
Take Some Risk

By the title of this chapter, you might think that I've lost my mind. That I'm going off the deep end by suggesting that you dabble in risky investments—purchase a bridge from your neighbor or speculate with biotech stocks or the next hot initial public offering.

No, not whatsoever. But it's true, I am suggesting that you take on more risk. This is to prevent a situation that could decimate your retirement income if you're not careful. I want you to take more risk and avoid being too conservative with your retirement portfolio.

Traditionally, as workers have neared retirement age, they gradually reduced their exposure to risk and favored more conservative investments. This doesn't always work out. An overly *conservative* investment strategy can be just as dangerous as one that is overly *aggressive*. A conservative strategy may expose your portfolio to the corrosive effects of inflation where prices increase and your purchasing power decreases. This raises the risk that you'll outlive your assets.

Inflation is insidious and can eat away at the purchasing power of your money. Even relatively low inflation can significantly impact a retiree's purchasing power over time. I notice the effects of inflation all the time. Do you? Just head over to the nearest sandwich shop and order a sandwich, chips, and drink. In my neck of the woods, it could cost more than $11 compared with $5 a few years ago. (Maybe I shouldn't get the chips . . .)

Yes, food, clothing, and other staples will cost more as you age. However, what concerns me most is the cost of medical care.

Not only are healthcare costs expensive and likely to change (i.e. Medicare), but these costs seem to rise at about double the rate of normal inflation. Genworth, the largest seller of long-term health insurance, reported that in 2013, the average cost of a private room in a nursing home was more than $83,000 per year. The Department of Health and Human Services states that the "average stay is two and a half years." That means you could find yourself spending $210,000 for care for yourself or a loved one. If you're lucky, you have a good long-term care (LTC) insurance policy. But given the recent sales numbers of long-term-care policies, that doesn't seem likely. In 2000, Americans purchased 750,000 new stand-alone, traditional LTC policies. That number was a paltry 105,000 in 2015, per the American Association for Long-Term Care Insurance.

Money magazine outs it this way:

> "Health care will likely be your biggest expense during the golden years. It's obviously a tough number to nail down and one that will vary by person, but there are estimates out there. A 65-year-old, healthy couple can expect to spend $266,600 over the course of their retirement on Medicare premiums alone, per HealthView Services."

If many of the rumored changes are made to Social Security and Medicare, the impact of medical costs might be even more profound. Much of this is outside of your control. But it leads me to an essential piece of guidance:

Take more risk in your investment portfolio! (Increase equity exposure)

An appropriate level depends on many factors. Over the long term, you'll need to have at least 30% of your retirement portfolio in equities. Depending on stock prices, it may make sense to have a bit more, or a bit less. Whatever the case, 100% bond portfolios won't get it done for you in the long run.

For best results, sprinkle in some equity exposure before and during your retirement to mitigate the insidious effects of inflation. Conservative investments won't outpace inflation.

That's just the way it works!

Chapter 26
Write It Down

Congrats on reaching the final stages of this book.

So, now you know the concept and you're intimately acquainted with the SECURiMENT Wheel. You know that peace of mind is achieved by aiming at the bullseye instead of one individual area.

Simply, you've learned that you must:

- Generate streams of income
- Reduce the volatility of your investments
- Use cash efficiently

Simple is good, right?

Unfortunately, SECURiMENT is not one size fits all and requires that you address many critical variables. Market risk, taxes, sources of income, long-term care, etc., are just a few examples, and all of this must be summarized in a **written retirement income plan.**

To me, the biggest factor of all is getting everything documented in a **written retirement income plan.** It makes sense. You don't spend assets in retirement; you spend income.

Your written retirement income plan should, at a minimum, answer these questions:

- Do you have a retirement income projection showing the total amount of income you can expect to receive every year throughout your entire retirement, broken down into each individual income source? Does your retirement income analysis show when each income source starts, stops, increases, and decreases?

- Do you have an income tax analysis showing how much income tax you will pay as you take income from your assets?

- Do you know how much money you can reasonably expect to leave to your beneficiaries after you've used your assets for income for your entire life?

- Do you have a written summary of your entire plan that includes the status of your current financial position, what you're trying to achieve, and the step-by-step process of what's required for success?

- Do you have an understanding of how much market exposure you have and what would happen if the market lost a ton of value?

For kicks, your plan should also cover something I refer to as **income sustainability**.

- How much income can you safely take out of your accounts?
- How long will your income last?
- Can you take out more income in the future?
- Is any part of your income guaranteed to be paid to you for as long as you (or both of you) live, and if not, what are your options to do so?

With regard to investments:

- How are you invested relative to your age and proximity to retirement?
- If the market drops 40%, how much will you lose?
- What amount of loss can you afford before it affects how long your money will last?
- Do you have any principal guarantees, or have you constructed a foundation (floor) under your assets?
- Are you taking enough risk?

This last one is interesting. Many people don't take enough

risk, and their returns are eaten up by inflation.

Sometimes, I feel that what is in the plan, in many ways, is secondary to simply having a *written* plan. Understanding how it all comes together is critical. Just because you will one day get tired of working doesn't mean that your bills will get tired of being paid.

That's just the way it works!

Chapter 26.2
The Final Straightaway

Congratulations, you have made it to the final straightaway of *The. Race. Of. Your. Life!* To refresh your memory, in the spirit of the marathon distance, there are 26.2 chapters in this book. How can there be .2 of a chapter? Good question. I'm happy to explain. You might call this part of the race The Final Straightaway. Every marathon has 26 miles and 385 yards and, often, it's those last steps that are the most challenging Without that Final Straightaway, it's not a marathon. It's mandatory; certainly, if you want a medal!

If you're resisting the urge to get started with your retirement planning, "The Final Straightaway" will help you. To examine this topic, we'll have to harken back to the marathon story I shared in the Introduction.

Remember the humiliation I suffered after having an extraordinarily early finish (not in a good way) in the Chicago Marathon? It was the day I stumbled upon this life-guiding nugget of how important it is to **have a plan** – whether for a race or for retirement. It doesn't have to be 300 pages long, but it does have to contemplate what you have now, what you'll need to retire the way you want, and, most importantly, a plan for getting there.

The following year, I tried the marathon distance again.

This time, I didn't tell quite as many people.

Despite running more leisurely, the results were the same. My day ended around 14 miles.

By now, my friends were having a field day with me. They would say things like "Did you see that nine-year-old girl cross the Finish Line? What an inspiration! You should run with her next year!" I tried one more time, but, in what was now a bad dream (or a full-blown nightmare), I experienced the same result. A short day and no medal! For some reason, I was unable to survive the middle miles. The part of the race where the excitement of the Start had faded, and you couldn't imagine the sweet victory of the Finish Line. You might be stuck in the middle miles. Knowing that your retirement plan needs work and that the clock is ticking, but unsure what to do.

That third year of marathon failure was flat-out demoralizing. I recalled the story of Pheidippides, the Greek messenger who dropped dead after running 26.2 miles to announce victory in the Battle of Marathon. Why, I thought, couldn't he have died after 14 miles instead? That shorter distance would then have become the definition of a marathon!

Anyway, after that last marathon flameout, I was devastated. I gave away all my running shoes, quit the sport in disgust, and wrote a sad, sad country song! (Let that one sink in . . .)

I spent several years away from the sport, but in 1997, my brother, Brian, valiantly completed his first Ironman Triathlon in Vancouver. It was a thrilling day because he covered about 140 miles by swimming, biking, and running. What did I do for exercise that day? I ran three miles – slowly; I even walked half the distance to boot. It was a low point in my decline from a runner who entered (but did not necessarily finish) a marathon every year to the couch potato I had become.

I didn't feel good about my sedentary lifestyle. My brother's success spurred me to give a marathon one more shot. However, I knew that this time I had to wake up and smell the Gatorade. I would have to change something about my approach to races if I wanted to experience different results!

The day before my brother's Ironman race, I had been reading about how successful athletes visualize the courses they run - mountains they ski, dirt paths they bike, etc. I came across a story that I've seen in numerous books and articles about an amazing Vietnam War veteran.

The Final Straightaway

> *Major James Nesbeth spent seven years as a prisoner of war in North Vietnam. During those seven years, he was imprisoned in a cage that was approximately four and one-half feet high and five long. During almost the entire time he was imprisoned he saw no one, talked to no one and experienced no physical activity. In order to keep his sanity and his mind active, he used the art of visualization. Every day in his mind, he would play a game of golf. A full 18-hole game at his favorite course. In his mind, he would create the trees, the smell of the freshly trimmed grass, the wind, the songs of the birds. He created different weather conditions - windy spring days, overcast winter days and sunny summer mornings. He felt the grip of the club in his hands as he played his shots in his mind. The set-up, the down-swing and the follow-through on each shot. Watched the ball arc down the fairway and land at the exact spot he had selected. All in his mind. He did this seven days a week. Four hours a day. Eighteen holes. Seven years. When Major Nesbeth was finally released, he found that he had cut 20 strokes off his golfing average without having touched a golf club in seven years.*

It was a compelling story. So, with all this information in mind, I set out to make a few changes. I figured there was nothing to lose. If Major Nesbeth, during his years of captivity, had managed to improve his golf game immensely merely by visualizing, the least I could do was find a way to see myself crawling across the Finish Line!

See the Finish Line

No matter where you're trying to go in retirement, if your goal is to live on your own terms or at your own pace, visualization may just be one of the most important tools you have at your disposal. Visualization is the practice of *seeing what you want*, so you're more likely *to get what you see.*

When I first began my training for running again, it was quite ugly. But as the weight came off, my legs began moving somewhat faster. With trepidation and a hint of sweaty palms,

The. Race. Of. Your. Life!

I mailed in the race application. But, even as I trained more frequently and saw my times improve, deep down I knew that something beyond this had to change. Getting off the couch was a significant first step. But if I prepared and executed as I had always done in the past, the outcome would be the same: NO FINISH! NO MEDAL!

Here's the change I made. Warning: it's going to get a bit bizarre!

The day before the race, I went to Grant Park in Chicago, the location of the Finish Line. I didn't go in work clothing or even training clothing. I went in race clothing: Running hat, shades, race T-shirt, and racing shorts that were probably, in retrospect, a bit too short. I attached my race number to my shirt, and I even wore a cheap medal I got from a local 5K race. That's how I planned to look the next day for the race!

Then it got weird. My wife was there with me and snapped photo after photo as I raised my arms in the air and let out a primal scream that might have woke up people living halfway around the world. I think some of the volunteers setting up for the following day may have thought the pre-race jitters had gotten the best of me. Someone nearby even asked if I was "ok" - which at that point was debatable!

Not to date myself, but we took the film to the local one-hour photo. So, an hour later, we had the picture she took of me standing under the Finish banner, before the race, celebrating the accomplishment I wanted so desperately to achieve. As I carbo-loaded that evening with a plateful of pasta, I glanced at the Finish Line photo. Before bed, I glanced at the photo. In the middle of the night, I glanced at the photo - and in the morning, as well. Right before the race began, I glanced at the photo. I saw the Finish Line.

With my eyes closed, I could see, hear, and feel the Finish Line. I could see the last few yards and the stands filled with cheering spectators. I could see the clock and the Finish banner overhead. I could hear the commotion and feel the asphalt

The Final Straightaway

under my feet. I could feel the weight of the finisher's medal around my neck. And as the race unfolded, my first revelation was that the doubt that had hampered me so often in previous attempts had taken the day off! Suddenly, the middle miles (the part of the race where the excitement of the Start had faded and you can't yet imagine the victory of the Finish Line) didn't loom so large. As the miles passed by, I realized, *"I'm getting closer and closer to the Finish Line! I'm surviving!"*

I passed the 14-mile mark!

I passed the 15-mile mark!

Then 20 miles were in the rear-view mirror!

Where was the WALL that I had heard so much about? The point in every marathoner's journey, where the body shuts down, usually around the 20-mile mark. But I didn't hit the WALL. Instead, I was enjoying the race (and getting a kick out of all the signs, including the one that read, "I'd follow you, if I could keep up!" and the person who shouted "SHUT UP LEGS!").

The visual I had internalized of finishing the race ended up blocking out all the negatives. Because the mind can only have one thought at a time, visions of cramps and abdominal distress were replaced by thoughts and sounds of adoring crowds and the visual of a large beverage after the race.

Then, 22 miles down!

The 25-mile marker was a thing of beauty! I felt great, but for others, it resembled the "walk of the living dead!" Runners were dropping like flies. Some were staggering, some were walking, and I even saw a few talking to themselves. Maybe they were promising their bodies they'd never, ever run this distance again, if they could just make it one more mile. I hit the final straightaway and never looked back. It wasn't like I was running on feathers, but it didn't feel like hot coals either!

When I crossed that Finish Line, I let out the primal scream of success that had escaped me in so many past marathons past. I'd been saving that one up for a long time!

Visualization Is Critical

Whether your goals are related to life or business, your health or relationships, a key principle remains the same: The distance between your reality and your aspirations will lessen if you put the image of achievement in your mind.

If you want to lose weight, picture buying a new outfit in a smaller size. See the tag. Envision yourself trying it on. Look in the mirror in the dressing room. You look good! Take a mental snapshot.

Similarly, if you want to retire with cash in the bank and fuel in the tank, picture yourself developing an effective retirement plan. Picture yourself traveling. Maybe you're on a cruise. No, not the one that was stranded for days and days in the middle of the ocean. Visualize a good one. You're in Mexico or the Caribbean. See the shows. Play Blackjack in the casino. Watch the sunset from the Promenade deck. Whatever the desire, see it. I can promise you this: If you visualize retirement success, you'll do a heck of a lot more to make it a reality.

This avenue of thinking works, regardless of the nature of your goal. Dreams are fuzzy. Dreams are ambiguous. And without having a crystal-clear vision, it's like saying I want to go on vacation to Greece, but not choosing the town. The odds are better you'll end up on Halsted in Greek Town than Athens — in the real Greece!

So formulate the future in your minds-eye and transition it to paper. Be explicit. Be clear. Be able to share the details in a moments notice!

You will get to the Finish Line. And I'll be waiting for you with a pat on the back or a banana. The choice is yours!

That's just the way it works!

About the Pandemic

You may have noticed there are only a few passing mentions of the Covid-19 pandemic in this book. No, I didn't live under a rock all those months, I lived in my house (all those months) and tried to keep my sanity.

Speaking of sanity, my favorite wife Jill and I recently made what we consider to be a sane decision to create more strength in our financial future. I'll share what we did in a moment.

Certainly, a book about retirement CANNOT ignore something as significant as a (hopefully) once in a lifetime event, so here are a few words about the pandemic as it may relate to your investments...

Upon reviewing and updating the last edition of this book, I left much of the material alone because, after boring myself with my thoughts, yet again...

...I felt that the lessons in the original text were still relevant.

Yes, the markets dropped significantly last Spring and Summer (2020), but the averages bounced right back and if you stayed invested, you were probably ok.

I continue to believe that the two other major declines this century (2000 – 2002) and (2007 – 2009) are better teaching lessons. For those declines it took much, much longer to get back to even.

But, alas, the events of the last several months were a learning experience for me as I'm sure they were for you. Just before the pandemic, I began using the words SAFETY, SIMPLICITY & STRENGTH in my teaching materials.

Over and over the same 3 words: SAFETY, SIMPLICITY & STRENGTH.

The. Race. Of. Your. Life!

I even went so far as to begin a class by saying if you're not going for safety, simplicity and strength in your financial life, you're on the wrong flight. (Like they used to do when you boarded an airplane.) In this case only one guy grabbed his carry on and exited the classroom…

Anyway, safety, simplicity and strength!

Safety is about being able to see the future with your eyes wide open. Too many employ the ostrich approach and stick their head in the sand or turn their back and pretend the clock isn't ticking. So, safety is not only about protecting your nest egg (in the conventional sense), but also about knowing what lurks around the corner.

Simplicity is about, well, keeping things simple. Here is an example of how simple our lives have been. Since March 2020, we've been focused on 1) Washing our hands (for more than 2.5 seconds), 2) Keeping our distance and 3) Wearing a mask even if it meant our glasses fogged up. (Not recommended while driving…)

Simple, right? (Oh, it got old after a while, but it wasn't complicated…)

Your retirement strategy should also be simple and concise. Just…

1) Protect your nest egg,
2) Create streams of income, and
3) Pay less income tax!

Of course, investment choices have complexity, but the overall strategy should be simple.

STRENGTH is about making uncomfortable decisions that may feel undesirable in the short term but offer the best chances for a favorable and comfortable long-term outcome.

Our difficult decision involved a big house with lots of empty bedrooms. Specifically, we were conflicted as to whether we should sell our house and downsize or stay put.

We ended up calling the moving company, but it was a gut-wrenching decision. For 25 years we have lived in the Deerfield community where we are adored by most everyone. That's a joke, but the reality is we have been very comfortable in Deerfield.

But now we don't need all that space and you know what they say – big house, big tax bill. With each passing day, it made less sense to stay.

As I type this in Spring, 2021, Josh and Danny are living in the city. Unfortunately, despite having moved on, their stuff is still all over the place in our current home. Is this some sort of gift for us? Do they think their possessions will disappear if they ignore them long enough?

[Boys, if you read this, please come visit! You can keep your junk here...]

Ben, our baby, is completing his first year at the University of Illinois and has a (virtual) internship this summer. He will be with us in our new Northbrook digs. Yes, our big move is the to the very community where both Jill and I grew up. The next one over. (We're a couple of thrill-seekers!)

Ok, here's the serious part.

The last year has taught me that anything can happen. Both personally and professionally.

My primary means of meeting prospective clients is by teaching classes. Although most end well past my bedtime, I still do so in the name of financial literacy and because they should teach this stuff in school. When it comes to helping people, I prefer to gain trust and build my business with an awkward mix of brains and quirkiness.

Can you guess how many classes I taught during the pandemic? Yep, you guessed it! ZERO!

Life can change in an instant.

Though remaining in our house was doable and the mortgage was low with an attractive, refinanced mortgage, staying would NOT have been operating from a position of STRENGTH.

Yes, it would have been much easier, but this last year taught me that a little discomfort now for more comfort later is a better play. So, we started packing. It's incredible; we've got so much stuff! Everything I tried to discard was apparently from Jill's grandma. I didn't realize she had 9 of them…

Now, as I type these words, we are fully ensconced in our new townhome. The basement is under construction so there is an exercise bike in the family room, but other than that we are LOVING it here.

Retirement can be complicated. It's the rest of your life after all! That doesn't mean how you approach it has to be.

So, there you have it. That's how the pandemic changed my thinking. Here is my final guidance for you. Stay safe, keep it simple and always flex your muscles by operating from a position of strength.

If you need help, I am here for you. As I always say…and this is really, really lame…you don't have to bulk up to have strength in retirement. SECURiMENT™ will do the heavy lifting for you!

I wish you the best of luck on the race of your life. I'll be rooting for you.

That's just the way it works!

After the Finish Line

Congratulations on finishing *The. Race. Of. Your. Life!* You made it a lot further than my three sons. They only skim my books to find material with which they can make fun of me! (By the way, here's a bonus lesson. Laugh at yourself! Life is hard enough if you can't laugh at yourself, so I do it all the time! Let's face it; there is much to make fun of...)

Now that you understand SECURiMENT and have some new strategies, resolve to be better today at managing and understanding your finances than yesterday. Aim to improve your situation, at least marginally, each day.

Does marginal improvement help? You bet it does. Consider this example. In the summer of 2010, the Chicago White Sox made a trade for pitcher Edwin Jackson. I remember the media (and fans) in Chicago were expecting a more substantial acquisition and described the White Sox as being (only) marginally better than before the trade. Ken Williams, White Sox general manager, correctly pointed out that most people (in most walks of life) would be thrilled (beyond compare) to be marginally better today than yesterday.

I agree, and it sure beats being marginally worse. Jackson, indeed, helped the White Sox. With him in the rotation, the team was better. Not World Series better, but better, nonetheless.

By the way, Edwin Jackson pitched for the Cubs a few years later and was absolutely dreadful. I could've gotten more batters out . . .)

But I digress.

Here's what I suggest that you do. Now that you've read through these lessons one time, re-open the book to any Lesson. Read it again—thoroughly. Examine whether you're currently

The. Race. Of. Your. Life!

doing what the lesson suggests. Take some notes. Ask whether or not your plan for retirement addresses what I've suggested in each chapter? If not, make some changes.

Don't focus on results at the outset. Instead, focus on small shifts. Or as retired Four-Star General Colin Powell suggests, "Do your best in the present."

Concentrate on your situation and resist the urge to compare yourself to others. While you're at it, stop comparing your investment performance to market averages. The performance you seek is a number that makes your plan work.

At the end of the day, you can't start where someone else is standing. You can only start from where you stand.

That's just the way it works.

About The Author

Darryl Rosen is the founder and chief retirement strategist at Retirement Info Chicago. A lifetime Chicagoan and former, somewhat competitive, but now washed up marathon runner, Darryl uses his experiences as a CPA, a successful business owner, a nationally known retirement strategist and a runner to help people plan for and achieve peace of mind in retirement.

He's also the undisputed and most world-renown expert on SECURiMENT, a word he created and uses to simplify the retirement planning process. Though he has created his own word, and people actually appreciate the concept, his children (and wife) are not even remotely impressed.

Darryl's clients enjoy his straight-forward guidance, strategies to minimize taxes in retirement and ability to generate investment returns, while minimizing risk. Darryl is licensed to provide guidance on securities and has achieved the highly desired Retirement Income Certified Professional (RICP) designation. He focuses not only on asset accumulation, but also on the de-accumulation of assets and creating a sustainable livelihood for clients in retirement.

Previously, Darryl spoke, trained, coached, consulted, and wrote on the subjects of leadership and culture, sales, management, and customer service. He is an experienced business professional and formerly served as President and Owner of Sam's Wines & Spirits, a $50 million multi-store retailer in the Chicago area.

Darryl earned an MBA in Marketing and Organizational Behavior from Northwestern University's Kellogg School of Management. He also holds a Bachelor's Degree in Accounting from Indiana University and is a Certified Public Accountant.

Darryl is also a graduate of the prestigious Canfield Training Group Train-The-Trainer Program. This highly selective, international program is designed to help human potential leaders teach and coach The Success Principles and equip future generations with skills needed to succeed.

He is the author of eight books on the topics of financial planning, sales, leadership, success, and effective management.

When he is not working, Darryl still enjoys running although he no longer runs marathons because, these days, making it to the end of the driveway is enough running. He also enjoys leisurely bike rides with his wife, Jill, whom he married because she was the first, and let's face it, the only girl who enjoyed speaking to him.

When not teaching or droning on obsessively about SECURiMENT, Darryl can be found checking his phone hoping Josh, Danny or Ben will text him for ANY other reason than wanting money! He is also a strong supporter of philanthropic efforts dedicated to feeding the hungry.

He's also a die-hard Chicago Cubs fan and hopes that this year will finally be the year that the Cubbies win the World Series, AGAIN!

For information about how Darryl can help you plan for a secure and comfortable retirement, contact him at darryl@roseadvisorygroup.com

Required Disclosure

This publication contains the opinions and ideas of its author. It is intended to provide helpful and informative material on the subject matter covered. It is sold with the understanding that the author and publisher are not engaged in rendering professional services in the book. The information provided is not intended as tax, investment or legal advice, and should not be relied on as such. If the reader requires personal assistance or advice, you are encouraged to seek tax, investment or legal advice from an independent professional advisor.
The author and publisher specifically disclaim any responsibility for any liability, loss, or risk, personal or otherwise, which is incurred as a consequence, directly or indirectly, of the use and application of any of the contents of this book.

Trademarks: All terms mentioned in this book that are known to be or are suspected of being trademarks or service marks have been appropriately capitalized. The publisher cannot attest to the accuracy of this information. Use of a term in this book should not be regarded as affecting the validity of any trademark or service mark.

Information provided in this book was prepared by Darryl Rosen. This book provides general information that is intended, but not guaranteed, to be correct and up-to-date information on the subjects discussed, and should not be regarded as a complete analysis of these subjects. You should not rely on statements or representations made within the book or by any externally referenced sources. No party assumes liability for any loss or damage resulting from errors or omissions or reliance on or use of this material.

The contents of this book should not be taken as financial advice, or as an offer to buy or sell any securities, fund, or financial instruments. Any illustrations or situations presented are hypothetical and do not take into account your particular investment objectives, financial situation or needs and are not suitable for all persons. Any investments and/or investment strategies mentioned involve risk including the possible loss of principal. There is no assurance that any investment strategy will achieve its objectives. No portion of the content should be construed as an offer or solicitation for the purchase or sale of any security. Any insurance products mentioned are guaranteed by the claims paying ability of the issuer and certain limitations and expenses may apply. The contents of this book should not be taken as an endorsement or recommendation of any particular company or individual, and no responsibility can be taken for inaccuracies, omissions, or errors.

The author does not assume any responsibility for actions or non-actions taken by people who have read this book, and no one shall be entitled to a claim for detrimental reliance based upon any information provided or expressed herein. Your use of any information provided does not constitute any type of contractual relationship between yourself and the provider(s) of this information. The author hereby disclaims all responsibility and liability for all use of any information provided in this book. The materials here are not to be interpreted as establishing an attorney-client or any other relationship between the reader and the author or his firm.

Although great effort has been expended to ensure that only the most meaningful resources are referenced in these pages, the author does not endorse, guarantee, or warranty the accuracy reliability, or thoroughness of any referenced information, product, or service. Any opinions, advice, statements, services, offers, or other information or content expressed or made available by third parties are those of the author(s) or publisher(s) alone. References to other sources of information does not constitute a referral, endorsement, or recommendation of any product or service. The existence of any particular reference is simply intended to imply potential interest to the reader.

The views expressed herein are exclusively those of the author and do not represent the views of any other person or any organization with which the author is, or may be associated.

www.ingramcontent.com/pod-product-compliance
Lightning Source LLC
Chambersburg PA
CBHW072030230526
45466CB00020B/1330